Whaddaya Say?

NINA WEINSTEIN

Guided Practice in Understanding Fast English

THIRD EDITION

Includes audio QR codes!

PROLINGUA LEARNING

DEDICATION

I dedicate this book to my son, Joshua.

Whaddaya Say? Guided Practice in Understanding Fast English, Third Edition
Copyright © 2025 Pro Lingua Learning
ISBN 978-0-86647-590-7

All rights reserved. No part of this book may be reproduced or transmitted in any form or by any means without permission in writing from the publisher. This restriction includes but is not limited to reproduction for educational and classroom purposes.

Pro Lingua Learning
PO Box 4467
Rockville, MD 20849
Orders: 800-888-4741 Main Office: 301-424-8900
www.ProLinguaLearning.com

Credits:
Editor: **Michael C. Berman**
Interior design: **Armin Castellón** and **Laura Guzman Aguilar**
Interior art: **Armin Castellón**
Cover design: **Laura Guzman Aguilar**

Special thanks to Michal Marell and Marilyn Rosenthal, PhD, for their editorial guidance.

Prior editions of this book were published by Pearson Education, Inc.

PRO LINGUA LEARNING

Contents

Introduction vii

1. **How's Your Family?** 1
   your, you're → *yer

2. **Yours is a Great Job!** 4
   yours → *yers

3. **I Have the Perfect Car for You** 7
   for → *fer

4. **Where Are the Bags of Chips?** 10
   of → *a

5. **Do You Like Artificial Intelligence?** 13
   you → *ya

6. **Let's Go Shopping** 16
   -ing endings → *-in'

7. **What Are You Doing This Weekend?** 19
   What do you, What are you → *Whaddaya

8. **I Want to Have a Hamburger** 22
   want to → *wanna

9. **We're Going to See "The Monster That Ate Cleveland"** 26
   going to + verb → *gonna

10. **Can You See the Stage?** 29
    can → *kin
    can't → can't (no change)

11. **What Can I Get You for Your Cold?** 32
    get → *git

12. **Take Bus 4 to Second Street** 35
    to → *ta

13. I'm Going to Try to Find a Job **38**
    to after a vowel sound ⟶ **da*

14. I've Got to Check Your Teeth **41**
    got to ⟶ **gotta*
    have to ⟶ **hafta*
    has to ⟶ **hasta*

15. She Used to Ride a Harley **44**
    used to ⟶ **useta*
    supposed to ⟶ **supposta*

16. What's the Fastest Way to Send His Packages? **48**
    he ⟶ **'e*
    his ⟶ **'is*
    him ⟶ **'im*
    her ⟶ **'er*
    them ⟶ **'em*

17. We Arrive on Tuesday and Leave on Thursday **52**
    and ⟶ **'n'*

18. Do You Want a Chocolate or Lemon Birthday Cake? **56**
    or ⟶ **er*

19. I Don't Know What Classes to Take **60**
    don't know ⟶ **donno*

20. Can't You Find an Apartment? **63**
    /t/ + *you* ⟶ **cha*
    /t/ + *your*
    /t/ + *you're* } ⟶ **cher*

21. Could You Check My Sink? **66**
    /d/ + *you* ⟶ **ja*
    /d/ + *your* ⟶ **jer*

22. Who Have You Asked to Fly the Plane? **70**
    Deletion of Initial /h/
    Wh- question words + have ⟶ **'ave*
    Wh- question words + has ⟶ **'as*
    Wh-question words + had ⟶ **'ad*

23. **Could I Have an Appointment with Dr. Okamoto?** **74**
Deletion of Initial /h/
Subject + *have* ⟶ *'ave
Subject + *has* ⟶ *'as
Subject + *had* ⟶ *'ad
Subject + *haven't* ⟶ *'aven't
Subject + *hasn't* ⟶ *'asn't
Subject + *hadn't* ⟶ *'adn't

24. **I Shouldn't Have Had Three Pieces of Cake** **78**

should ⎫
could ⎪
would ⎬ + *have* + past participle ⟶ ⎧ *shoulda
must ⎪   ⎪ *coulda
may ⎪   ⎪ *woulda
might ⎭   ⎨ *musta
                                        ⎪ *maya
                                        ⎩ *mighta

shouldn't ⎫
couldn't ⎬ + *have* + past participle ⟶ ⎧ *shouldna
wouldn't ⎭   ⎨ *couldna
                                        ⎩ *wouldna

25. **What Are You Doing to My Hair?** **82**
Very Informal Reduction
What are you ⟶ *Whacha

26. **Give Me a Paintbrush** **86**
Very Informal Reductions
let me ⟶ *lemme
give me ⟶ *gimme

27. **I Couldn't Take the Test Because I Was Sick** **90**
Deletion of Syllables
about ⟶ *'bout
because ⟶ *cause
come on ⟶ *c'mon

28. **Been to the Circus Lately?** **94**
Deletion of Words in Questions
Do you want some ⟶ *Want some...*
Are you going to see... ⟶ *Gonna see...
Would you like to ... ⟶ *Like to...*
Have you seen the... ⟶ *Seen the...*

29. Where Are Your Extra-Large Hats? **98**
Unusual Contractions
What are ⟶ *What're
What will ⟶ *What'll
Where are ⟶ *Where're
Where will ⟶ *Where'll
Why are ⟶ *Why're
Why will ⟶ *Why'll

30. When Will Your TV Program Be Over? **102**
Unusual Contractions
Who are ⟶ *Who're
Who will ⟶ *Who'll
When are ⟶ *When're
When will ⟶ *When'll
How are ⟶ *How're
How will ⟶ *How'll

Test Yourself **106**

Test Yourself Audio Script **109**

Test Yourself Answer Key **111**

Chapter Answer Key **112**

Alternate Levels of Reductions **119**

Sentence Blending Rules **120**

Conversational Strategies **121**

Introduction

Whaddaya Say? Third Edition **(WS3)** updates the second edition, which was the result of twenty-five years of research on reduced forms. In addition to being an easy-to-use listening book that teaches the most common reduced forms (*wanna, *gonna, *gotta, etc.) needed to understand natural spoken English, WS3 presents each reduced form fully contextualized in practical, fun conversations.

Reduced forms are the pronunciation changes that occur in natural speech because of the environment or context in which a word or sound is found. The amount of reduction (the level) depends on how fast the word or sound is spoken.

Example:

SLOW SPEECH	**FASTER**	**FASTEST**
Level 1: *want to*	Level 2: *want *ta*	Level 3: **wanna*

WS3 focuses on Level 3 reduced forms because, according to research, this level is by far the most common. A detailed list of reductions that have three or more levels is included at the end of WS3, on page 119.

What's New to the Third Edition of WS3?

In general, all of the features that have made *Whaddaya Say?* so successful over the years have been maintained, and we have made some important updates to make it even more relevant and easy to use.

- **Audio QR Codes to Access the Digital Audio Program**
  We have included a QR code next to every listening-based activity in the book, allowing users to access the precise audio segment instantly and without extra hassle or cost. The QR codes can also access the audio for the Test Yourself program at the back of the book.

- **Updated Versions of Chapters 5, 8, 10, 24 and 29**
  These chapters have been revised to bring the content up to date while still covering the same essential reductions in fast and slow speech.

- **Sentence Blending Rules**
  This new appendix presents three main sentence blending rules with examples. These guidelines further build students' skills in understanding fast English.

- **Conversational Strategies**
  In the new "Conversational Strategies" appendix, the author provides a list of common words, short phrases, and rejoinders that are used by native speakers to maintain a conversation.

Design of the Chapters

Each chapter follows the same outline as shown below. At the top of each opening page, there is a silhouette illustration suggesting the theme or type of conversation. On the top right of the opening page, readers can see the teaching point showing the full form and reduced form that is treated in the given chapter. These elements can be used as a warm-up for previewing the conversation and teaching point for the students. Generally, each chapter represents about 50 minutes of presentation and practice material.

Part 1: Introduction

- **Conversation**
  In the conversations, learners are introduced to the reduced forms for that lesson. After Chapter 1, previously learned reduced forms are recycled in the conversations and throughout the chapters. For this reason, as learners progress through the chapters, the conversations become more and more like the spoken English they'll hear in the real world. Learners first listen to a segment of a conversation spoken with careful, slow pronunciation. They contrast this pronunciation with the same segment spoken with relaxed, fast speech that uses the target reduced forms. Afterward, the entire conversation is repeated using only relaxed, fast speech. Depending on their abilities, learners can follow along in their books or listen with their books closed.

  To remind learners that the reduced forms are not to be used for written English, an asterisk (*) is used with every reduced form.

- **Comprehension**
  The Comprehension questions check learners' basic understanding of the conversation. Some questions ask learners to form opinions. Learners can compare answers with a partner at the end of the exercise, and then share their answers with the class.

- **Practice**
  Learners' books should be closed for the Practice section. This is basically a translation exercise in which learners repeat only the slow, careful pronunciation of the relaxed, fast speech they hear. If learners have difficulty, they can stop the audio after each sentence to allow them to "translate" it from natural spoken English to the written English in smaller, easier chunks.

Part 2: Expansion

- **Comprehension**
  In this part, learners hear a new conversation, usually a continuation of the opening conversation, but spoken in the relaxed, fast pronunciation of the real world. The Comprehension questions can be used to ensure that learners understand the key points of the second conversation. If learners have difficulty answering these questions, they can listen to the audio again. If learners have difficulty understanding this conversation in the audio program, they can open their books to the Part 2 Practice section and follow along.

- **Practice**

In this section, learners listen to the Part 2 conversation again, filling in the blanks with the missing reduced forms. They should use the conventional spellings of the reduced forms that they hear. For example, if they hear *n, they should write *and*. After learners have filled in all of the blanks, they listen again and check their answers before sharing the correct answers with the class.

- **Discussion**

  Learners can work in small groups to discuss the final questions on the chapter topic. The purpose of this section is to encourage learners to bring their own experiences into the classroom and into their discussion of the chapter topic.

Test Yourself

Ten review tests for easily confused reduced forms appear at the back of the book (pages 106-108). Each test consists of a short conversation featuring the target reduced forms. This section also includes a tapescript and answer key for each self-test. Learners should take each test after they finish the chapter that appears next to it. If learners have difficulty with a particular test, they should re-do the chapters with the reduced forms that caused the difficulty. Learners can also do the entire Test Yourself section when they finish WS3 to reinforce their understanding of natural spoken English.

Should Learners Use Reduced Forms in Their Own Speech?

Throughout the various editions of *Whaddaya Say?* and my interactions with learners all over the world, learners have wondered if they should use reduced forms in their own speech to sound more like native English speakers.

Here's my best answer. WS3 is a listening book. Learners must be able to understand English speakers as they really speak, which is what WS3 teaches. However, as the book became so universally used, I found that learners were using *Whaddaya Say?* for accent reduction.

All of the reduced forms in WS3 are natural and common. Remember, reduced forms are caused by speed of speech, but because they're caused by speed of speech, for learners to sound natural, they have to speak at the speed that caused the reduced forms. This can be difficult as learners learn more reduced forms.

Here's the fast, easy fix that I teach my own learners. All of the reduced forms in WS3 are common, but there are three that are the most popular. They are *wanna, *gonna, and *hafta. In formal research at UCLA, I found that one of these forms is said about every two minutes. That means if learners use just these three, which are very easy to pronounce, it will sound like the learner is using a lot of reduced forms because of the frequency of these reductions. That will instantly naturalize non-native, English speakers' speech.

Acknowledgements

I'd like to thank Michael Berman, Chief Education Officer of Pro Lingua Learning, for his careful comments on *Whaddaya Say? Third Edition*.

I'd also like to thank the many thousands of learners all over the world who have successfully learned to understand real spoken English from *Whaddaya Say?*

1 How's Your Family?

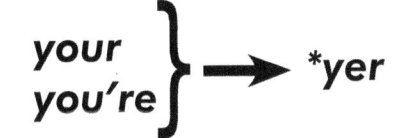

$$\left.\begin{array}{c}\textit{your}\\ \textit{you're}\end{array}\right\} \rightarrow \textit{*yer}$$

Your and *you're* aren't pronounced *yer* if stressed.

Part 1 INTRODUCTION

CONVERSATION

Listen to each part of the conversation: first spoken with careful (slow) pronunciation, then spoken with relaxed (fast) pronunciation.

Careful (Slow) Pronunciation

CARLOS: Maria? Maria Gonzalez? My gosh! You're so tall now.
MARIA: Carlos! My old neighbor! Wow! You're looking great.
CARLOS: Thanks. So ...how's your family?
MARIA: They're fine. How about *your* family?
CARLOS: They're fine, too.
MARIA: That's good. Does your mother still volunteer at a school?
CARLOS: Yes, she does.
MARIA: That's great. Your mother's a really nice person.
CARLOS: You're right. She is. So, does your father still sing with his friends?
MARIA: Every weekend.

Relaxed (Fast) Pronunciation

CARLOS: Maria? Maria Gonzalez? My gosh! *Yer so tall now.
MARIA: Carlos! My old neighbor! Wow! *Yer looking great.
CARLOS: Thanks. So... how's *yer family?
MARIA: They're fine. How about *your* family?
CARLOS: They're fine, too.
MARIA: That's good. Does *yer mother still volunteer at a school?
CARLOS: Yes, she does.
MARIA: That's great. *Yer mother's a really nice person.
CARLOS: *Yer right. She is. So, does *yer father still sing with his friends?
MARIA: Every weekend.

TRACK 1A

Listen to the entire conversation again, spoken with relaxed (fast) pronunciation.

TRACK 1B

How's Your Family? **1**

COMPREHENSION

Answer these questions about the conversation.

1. What's the relationship between Maria and Carlos?
2. How often do you think they see each other? Explain.
3. What do you know about each family?
4. What do you think Carlos' mother does at the school?
5. Where do you think Maria's father sings every weekend?

Now, work with a partner and compare your answers.

PRACTICE

Close your book. You'll hear each part of the conversation spoken with relaxed pronunciation. Repeat each part using careful pronunciation.

TRACK 1C

Part 2 EXPANSION

COMPREHENSION

Listen to the conversation. The speakers use relaxed pronunciation. Answer the questions.

1. Which family moved? When?
2. What do you know about Carlos' sister and Maria's brother?
3. Which family members don't know about the marriage plans?
4. Why do you think some family members don't know?
5. Do you think Carlos wants his sister to marry Maria's brother? Explain.
6. Should Carlos and Maria tell their parents about the marriage plans? Explain.
7. The best title for this conversation is
   a. Good Friends   b. An Exciting Marriage   c. Invite Me to the Divorce   d. Other _____

Work with a partner. Compare your answers. Listen again if necessary.

TRACK 1D

PRACTICE

Listen again. The conversation is spoken with relaxed pronunciation. Complete the sentences with the words you would hear if they were spoken with careful pronunciation. Then, listen once more and check your answers.

TRACK 1E

MARIA: Carlos, _____(1)_____ family moved two years ago, right?

CARLOS: Yes.

MARIA: _____(2)_____ twenty now?

CARLOS: Yes. And _____(3)_____ seventeen?

MARIA: No. Eighteen.

CARLOS: Oh. _____(4)_____ a mechanic now, right?

MARIA: That's right. So ... _____(5)_____ sister is a doctor in the Peace Corps, isn't she?

CARLOS: Uh huh. Is _____(6)_____ brother still an actor in Hollywood?

MARIA: Yeah. He does a soap commercial on TV. He e-mails _____(7)_____ sister every day.

CARLOS: Do _____(8)_____ parents know they plan to get married?

MARIA: No. Do _____(9)_____ parents know?

CARLOS: I don't think so. _____(10)_____ brother and my sister have really different lives.

MARIA: _____(11)_____ not happy about their engagement?

CARLOS: I'm just worried. They're so different.

MARIA: _____(12)_____ right. They are.

DISCUSSION

Work in small groups.

Is it better for a husband and wife to be interested in the same things? Explain.

2 Yours Is a Great Job!

yours → *yers

Part 1 INTRODUCTION

CONVERSATION

Listen to each part of the conversation: first spoken with careful (slow) pronunciation, then spoken with relaxed (fast) pronunciation.

Careful (Slow) Pronunciation	Relaxed (Fast) Pronunciation
LINDA: I just got a raise at work.	LINDA: I just got a raise at work.
TIM: Really? I love your job.	TIM: Really? I love *yer job.
LINDA: I love yours.	LINDA: I love *yers.
TIM: Your job pays really well.	TIM: *Yer job pays really well.
LINDA: Yours is interesting.	LINDA: *Yers is interesting.
TIM: Your boss teaches the employees new things.	TIM: *Yer boss teaches the employees new things.
LINDA: But yours is funny.	LINDA: But *yers is funny.
TIM: You're right, but your job is near your home.	TIM: *Yer right, but *yer job is near *yer home.
LINDA: Yours is near your father-in-law's house.	LINDA: *Yers is near *yer father-in-law's house.
TIM: Yeah. Yours is far from my father-in-law's house... I love your job.	TIM: Yeah. *Yers is far from my father-in-law's house... I love *yer job.

TRACK 2A

Listen to the entire conversation again, spoken with relaxed (fast) pronunciation.

TRACK 2B

4 Chapter 2

COMPREHENSION

Answer these questions about the conversation.

1. Who got a raise?
2. What do you know about Linda's job?
3. What do you know about Tim's job?
4. Do you think Tim likes his father-in-law? Explain.

Now, work with a partner and compare your answers.

PRACTICE

Close your book. You'll hear each part of the conversation spoken with relaxed pronunciation. Repeat each part using careful pronunciation.

TRACK 2C

Part 2 EXPANSION

COMPREHENSION

Listen to the conversation. The speakers use relaxed pronunciation. Answer the questions.

1. What's Tim's problem?
2. How do you think he feels about the problem?
3. What does Linda like about Tim's job?
4. What does Tim like about Linda's job?
5. Guess what Tim's job is. Explain.
6. Guess what Linda's job is. Explain.

Work with a partner. Compare your answers. Listen again if necessary.

TRACK 2D

Yours Is a Great Job! 5

PRACTICE

Listen again. The conversation is spoken with relaxed pronunciation. Complete the sentences with the words you would hear if they were spoken with careful pronunciation. Then, listen once more and check your answers.

TIM: I didn't get a raise.

LINDA: Oh, Tim. I'm really sorry. But _____1_____ is a great job.

TIM: It doesn't pay very well.

LINDA: _____2_____ job helps people. That's important.

TIM: _____3_____ right, but _____4_____ pays well.

LINDA: Money isn't everything. _____5_____ co-workers are nice.

TIM: _____6_____ are really intelligent.

LINDA: So are _____7_____ .

TIM: _____8_____ job is fun.

LINDA: _____9_____ isn't fun?

TIM: Yeah, _____10_____ right. _____11_____ pays better, but my job is really fun.

DISCUSSION

Work in small groups.

Which is more important in a job: to make good money, to help people, or to have fun? Explain.

3 I Have the Perfect Car for You

for ⟶ *fer

For doesn't become ***fer** if stressed or if it's not followed by another word. Example: Who's this *for*?

Part 1 INTRODUCTION

CONVERSATION

Listen to each part of the conversation: first spoken with careful (slow) pronunciation, then spoken with relaxed (fast) pronunciation.

TRACK 3A

Careful (Slow) Pronunciation	Relaxed (Fast) Pronunciation

JOHN: I'm looking for a car.
SALESPERSON: Okay. For a new car?
JOHN: No. For a used car.
SALESPERSON: For a recent model?
JOHN: Yes. For a late model economy car.
SALESPERSON: What price do you have in mind for the car?
JOHN: Around $8,500. What's your price range for economy cars?
SALESPERSON: You can't buy a late model for $8,500.
JOHN: You're sure?
SALESPERSON: Yes, sir. But I have a very nice late model for $11,900.

JOHN: I'm looking *fer a car.
SALESPERSON: Okay. *Fer a new car?
JOHN: No. *Fer a used car.
SALESPERSON: *Fer a recent model?
JOHN: Yes. *Fer a late model economy car.
SALESPERSON: What price do you have in mind *fer the car?
JOHN: Around $8,500. What's *yer price range *fer economy cars?
SALESPERSON: You can't buy a late model *fer $8,500.
JOHN: *Yer sure?
SALESPERSON: Yes, sir. But I have a very nice late model *fer $11,900.

Listen to the entire conversation again, spoken with relaxed (fast) pronunciation.

TRACK 3B

COMPREHENSION

Answer these questions about the conversation.

1. What kind of car is John looking for?
2. How much does he want to spend?
3. Do you think this is enough money to buy a late model car? Explain.
4. Does the salesperson think this is enough money? Explain.
5. What does the salesperson offer John?
6. What do you think John will say next?

Now, work with a partner and compare your answers.

PRACTICE

Close your book. You'll hear each part of the conversation spoken with relaxed pronunciation. Repeat each part using careful pronunciation.

TRACK 3C

Part 2 EXPANSION

COMPREHENSION

Listen to the conversation. The speakers use relaxed pronunciation. Answer the questions.

1. Is John happy when he sees the car? Explain.
2. What does the salesperson say about each problem with the car?
3. What would John have to do to fix the car?
4. Would you buy a car from this salesperson? Why or why not?

Work with a partner. Compare your answers. Listen again if necessary.

TRACK 3D

8   Chapter 3

PRACTICE

Listen again. The conversation is spoken with relaxed pronunciation. Complete the sentences with the words you would hear if they were spoken with careful pronunciation. Then, listen once more and check your answers.

TRACK 3E

SALESPERSON: Looking _____(1)_____ a car, sir?

JOHN: Yes. _____(2)_____ a used car.

SALESPERSON: _____(3)_____ a used car? _____(4)_____ in the right place.

JOHN: A late model economy car _____(5)_____ city driving. It's _____(6)_____ my family.

SALESPERSON: Say no more. I have the perfect car _____(7)_____ city driving. _____(8)_____ family will love it. Follow me.

JOHN: Is *this* it?

SALESPERSON: This is the one. Isn't it beautiful?

JOHN: But the paint's chipped.

SALESPERSON: No problem. _____(9)_____ a few extra dollars, we'll fix that _____(10)_____ you. It'll look just like new.

JOHN: How many miles has it got?

SALESPERSON: Oh, around 95,000. But _____(11)_____ a few extra dollars, we'll rebuild the engine. It'll be just like new.

JOHN: The tires are bald.

SALESPERSON: _____(12)_____ right. But _____(13)_____ a few more dollars, we'll put on new tires. This will be a beautiful car _____(14)_____ _____(15)_____ family.

DISCUSSION

Work in small groups.

Compare this salesperson to other salespeople that you've met.

I Have the Perfect Car For You   9

4 Where Are the Bags of Chips?

of ⟶ *a

Of doesn't become **a* if stressed, or if it's not followed by another word. Example:
A: Is it 3:00?
B: No. It´s ten **of**.

Part 1 INTRODUCTION

CONVERSATION

Listen to each part of the conversation: first spoken with careful (slow) pronunciation, then spoken with relaxed (fast) pronunciation.

Careful (Slow) Pronunciation	Relaxed (Fast) Pronunciation
JULIE: The party's tonight. I've invited a lot of people.	JULIE: The party's tonight. I've invited a lot *a people.
SHOKO: Then, let's go shopping. It's already a quarter of three.	SHOKO: Then, let's go shopping. It's already a quarter *a three.
JULIE: You're right. It's late. Let's make a list.	JULIE: *Yer right. It's late. Let's make a list.
SHOKO: Okay. We need a case of soda.	SHOKO: Okay. We need a case *a soda.
JULIE: Right. We also need a bag of pretzels.	JULIE: Right. We also need a bag *a pretzels.
SHOKO: What about a few bags of chips?	SHOKO: What about a few bags *a chips?
JULIE: Okay. And a couple of packages of cheese for the dip.	JULIE: Okay. And a couple *a packages *a cheese *fer the dip.
SHOKO: Great. Your cheese dips are always so good.	SHOKO: Great. *Yer cheese dips are always so good.
JULIE: Thanks. We need a couple of other things, too.	JULIE: Thanks. We need a couple *a other things, too.
SHOKO: Wait. I don't have my credit card. Do you have yours?	SHOKO: Wait. I don't have my credit card. Do you have *yers?

TRACK 4A

Listen to the entire conversation again, spoken with relaxed (fast) pronunciation.

TRACK 4B

10 Chapter 4

COMPREHENSION

Answer these questions about the conversation.

1. What are Julie and Shoko planning to do? When?
2. What do you think their relationship is?
3. How much cheese will they buy?
4. What other food do they need?
5. Who will pay for the food? Why?
6. Do you think they planned well for the party? Explain.

Now, work with a partner and compare your answers.

PRACTICE

Close your book. You'll hear each part of the conversation spoken with relaxed pronunciation. Repeat each part using careful pronunciation.

TRACK 4C

Part 2 EXPANSION

COMPREHENSION

Listen to the conversation. The speakers use relaxed pronunciation. Answer the questions.

1. What food does Julie buy?
2. In which aisles does she find each kind of food?
3. Do you think Julie's party food is nutritious? Explain.
4. What party food would be more nutritious?
5. What time is the party?
6. What does Julie need to do before the party?

Work with a partner. Compare your answers. Listen again if necessary.

Where Are the Bags of Chips? **11**

PRACTICE

Listen again. The conversation is spoken with relaxed pronunciation. Complete the sentences with the words you would hear if they were spoken with careful pronunciation. Then, listen once more and check your answers.

TRACK 4E

JULIE: Excuse me. Where's the milk?

CHECKER: It's down aisle 15.

JULIE: Thanks.

CHECKER: Excuse me, Miss. _____(1)_____ going the wrong way. Aisle 15 is on _____(2)_____ left.

JULIE: Oh! Thank you. *(to herself)* I need three cartons _____(3)_____ milk and a few cartons _____(4)_____ orange juice.

(to clerk) Excuse me. Where are the boxes _____(5)_____ cookies?

CLERK: Go down aisle 10. They're at the end _____(6)_____ the aisle. They're beside the cans _____(7)_____ nuts.

JULIE: Thanks. Oh! I also want meat _____(8)_____ hamburgers. Where's the meat section?

CLERK: It's at the end _____(9)_____ aisle 1. Aisle 1 is on _____(10)_____ right, in the corner _____(11)_____ the store.

JULIE: One more thing. I need buns _____(12)_____ the hamburgers.

CLERK: Hamburger buns are at the end _____(13)_____ aisle 2, near the crackers.

JULIE: Thank you *(to another shopper)* Excuse me. What time is it?

SHOPPER: It's ten _____(14)_____ four.

JULIE: *(to herself)* Oh, my gosh! I need to make all _____(15)_____ the food _____(16)_____ the party in two hours!

DISCUSSION

Work in small groups.

What food do you usually have at parties? Discuss.

5 Do You Like Artificial Intelligence?

you ⟶ *ya

You isn't pronounced **ya* if stressed.

Part 1 INTRODUCTION

CONVERSATION

Listen to each part of the conversation: first spoken with careful (slow) pronunciation; then spoken with relaxed (fast) pronunciation.

Careful (Slow) Pronunciation	Relaxed (Fast) Pronunciation
JOSH: Grandpa, do you like this new AI website?	JOSH: Grandpa, do *ya like this new AI website?
GRANDPA: Huh?	GRANDPA: Huh?
JOSH: Do you know how to use it?	JOSH: Do *ya know how to use it?
GRANDPA: Well, no. Do *you*?	GRANDPA: Well, no. Do *you*?
JOSH: Sure. I'll show you. It'll just take a couple of minutes.	JOSH: Sure. I'll show *ya. It'll just take a couple *a minutes.
GRANDPA: No, thanks. AI is for young people.	GRANDPA: No, thanks. AI is *fer young people.
JOSH: AI is for everybody.	JOSH: AI is *fer everybody.
GRANDPA: Okay. How do you use AI?	GRANDPA: Okay. How do *ya use AI?
JOSH: Well, first, you type in your prompt.	JOSH: Well, first, *ya type in *yer prompt.
GRANDPA: Prompt? What are you talking about?	GRANDPA: Prompt? What are *ya talking about?

TRACK 5A

Listen to the entire conversation again, spoken with relaxed (fast) pronunciation.

TRACK 5B

Do You Like Artificial Intelligence? **13**

COMPREHENSION

Answer these questions about the conversation.

1. How old do you think Josh's grandfather is? Why?
2. How old do you think Josh is? Why?
3. Do you think his grandfather has used AI before? Explain.
4. Is his grandfather interested in AI? Explain.

Now, work with a partner and compare your answers.

PRACTICE

Close your book. You'll hear each part of the conversation spoken with relaxed pronunciation. Repeat each part using careful pronunciation.

TRACK 5C

Part 2 EXPANSION

COMPREHENSION

Listen to the conversation. The speakers use relaxed pronunciation. Answer the questions.

1. Is Josh's grandfather interested in AI at first?
2. Why does Josh's grandfather say, "You're almost ready to retire and buy a home in Florida"? Is he serious?
3. How does Josh's grandfather feel about AI by the end of the conversation?

Work with a partner. Compare your answers. Listen again if necessary.

TRACK 5D

PRACTICE

Listen again. The conversation is spoken with relaxed pronunciation. Complete the sentences with the words you would hear if they were spoken with careful pronunciation. Then, listen once more and check your answers.

TRACK 5E

GRANDPA: Let's do something fun today. Let's stream a soccer movie.

JOSH: Yeah! But let me teach _____(1) about AI first!

GRANDPA: Now?

JOSH: Yeah! Why not? Okay, first _____(2) decide _____(3) question. Ask the AI site _____(4) the best soccer movies. Then tell it who _____(5) are. _____(6) could tell it _____(7) a soccer movie fan and his grandson.

GRANDPA: _____(8) just a child. How do _____(9) know so much about AI?

JOSH: Grandpa, I'm ten years old, _____(10) know!

GRANDPA: Right. _____(11) ten years old. _____(12) almost ready to retire and buy a home in Florida.

JOSH: Very funny, Grandpa.

GRANDPA: Look at this! AI gives _____(13) information about all _____(14) the best soccer movies!

(Twenty minutes later)

JOSH: Grandpa, are _____(15) *still* on the AI website? When will _____(16) be ready to see the movie?

DISCUSSION

Work in small groups.

Do you know many elderly people who like the latest technology? What do you think is the most interesting part of AI? Explain.

Do You Like Artificial Intelligence?

6 Let's Go Shopping

> **-ing endings ⟶ *-in'**
>
> Most native English speakers do not use the *-in' pronunciation for all -ing endings. The *-in' pronunciation is most often used with continuous verb tenses. The *-in' pronunciation is very informal.

Part 1 INTRODUCTION

CONVERSATION

Listen to each part of the conversation: first spoken with careful (slow) pronunciation, then spoken with relaxed (fast) pronunciation.

Careful (Slow) Pronunciation	Relaxed (Fast) Pronunciation
NANCY: Well, hi! You're shopping here, too!	NANCY: Well, hi! *Yer *shoppin' here, too!
KIM: Not really. I'm just looking around. So, how have you been?	KIM: Not really. I'm just *lookin' around. So, how have *ya been?
NANCY: Great. I'm shopping with my sister. She's over there.	NANCY: Great. I'm *shoppin' with my sister. She's over there.
KIM: Is that your sister? The tall woman in front of the jackets?	KIM: Is that *yer sister? The tall woman in front *a the jackets?
NANCY: Yes. She's looking for a jacket for work.	NANCY: Yes. She's *lookin' *fer a jacket *fer work.
KIM: Are you shopping for work clothes, too?	KIM: Are *ya *shoppin' *fer work clothes, too?
NANCY: No. I'm looking for a pair of jeans like yours.	NANCY: No. I'm *lookin' *fer a pair *a jeans like *yers.
KIM: Oh. I found these here last week for 30 percent off.	KIM: Oh. I found these here last week *fer 30 percent off.
NANCY: For 30 percent off? Thanks for telling me.	NANCY: *Fer 30 percent off? Thanks *fer *tellin' me.
KIM: Well nice seeing you again. I hope you find what you're looking for.	KIM: Well nice seein' *ya again. I hope *ya find what *yer *lookin' for.

TRACK 6A

Listen to the entire conversation again, spoken with relaxed (fast) pronunciation.

TRACK 6B

COMPREHENSION

Answer these questions about the conversation.

1. What's Nancy doing?
2. How does Nancy greet Kim?
3. What are other ways to greet someone?
4. How well do you think Nancy and Kim know each other? Explain.
5. Why does Nancy thank Kim?
6. How does Kim say "good-bye"?
7. What are other ways to say "good-bye" in this situation?

Now, work with a partner and compare your answers.

PRACTICE

Close your book. You'll hear each part of the conversation spoken with relaxed pronunciation. Repeat each part using careful pronunciation.

TRACK 6C

Part 2 EXPANSION

COMPREHENSION

Listen to the conversation. The speakers use relaxed pronunciation. Answer the questions.

1. What kind of jeans does Nancy want?
2. Does Nancy know where the dressing room is at first? Explain.
3. How does she ask for more information about the dressing room?
4. What are other ways to ask for more information if you don't understand something?
5. Does Nancy like the fitted jeans? Explain.
6. Why does the salesperson suggest designer jeans?
7. What do you think Nancy will say next?

Work with a partner. Compare your answers. Listen again if necessary.

TRACK 6D

Let's Go Shopping 17

PRACTICE

Listen again. The conversation is spoken with relaxed pronunciation. Complete the sentences with the words you would hear if they were spoken with careful pronunciation. Then, listen once more and check your answers.

TRACK 6E

SALESPERSON: May I help _____(1)_____ ?

NANCY: Yes. I'm _____(2)_____ _____(3)_____ some jeans.

SALESPERSON: Are _____(4)_____ _____(5)_____ _____(6)_____ fitted jeans, baggy jeans...

NANCY: Fitted jeans in a size 12.

SALESPERSON: We have two styles in _____(7)_____ size. Here _____(8)_____ are. Why don't _____(9)_____ try them on in the dressing room over there?

NANCY: Excuse me. *Where's* the dressing room?

SALESPERSON: Over there. In the corner _____(10)_____ the store, on _____(11)_____ right.

(A few minutes later)

SALESPERSON: So, how were they?

NANCY: They were a little big, but that's okay. I'm really _____(12)_____ _____(13)_____ dressier jeans. _____(14)_____ _____(15)_____ to a play, _____(16)_____ to a movie...

SALESPERSON: Dressy jeans... Well, _____(17)_____ might be interested in _____(18)_____ a look at our designer jeans. A lot _____(19)_____ people are _____(20)_____ designer jeans _____(21)_____ evening wear.

NANCY: Okay. Where are they?

SALESPERSON: Behind _____(22)_____. _____(23)_____ _____(24)_____ right in front _____(25)_____ them.

DISCUSSION

Work in small groups.

What do people you know wear to go out at night? Discuss.

18 Chapter 6

7 What Are You Doing This Weekend?

> What do you } → *Whaddaya
> What are you }
>
> A related form, *Whadda,* is used when *What do* is followed by either *we* or *they*. Examples:
>
> *Whadda* we need?
> *Whadda* they want?

Part 1 INTRODUCTION

CONVERSATION

Listen to each part of the conversation: first spoken with careful (slow) pronunciation, then spoken with relaxed (fast) pronunciation.

Careful (Slow) Pronunciation

KENJI: What are you doing this weekend?
TIM: Not much. What do you have in mind?
KENJI: Bungee jumping.
TIM: Bungee jumping?
KENJI: What do you think?
TIM: Maybe. What do we need to bring?
KENJI: What do we need? Well, a couple of bottles of water, some backpacks…
TIM: What are you thinking of having for food?
KENJI: Oh, fried egg sandwiches, chocolate cake, soda… What are you doing?
TIM: I'm writing it down.

Relaxed (Fast) Pronunciation

KENJI: *Whaddaya *doin' this weekend?
TIM: Not much. *Whaddaya have in mind?
KENJI: Bungee jumping.
TIM: Bungee jumping?
KENJI: *Whaddaya think?
TIM: Maybe. *Whadda we need to bring?
KENJI: *Whadda we need? Well, a couple *a bottles *a water, some backpacks…
TIM: *Whaddaya *thinkin' *a *havin' *fer food?
KENJI: Oh, fried egg sandwiches, chocolate cake, soda… *Whaddaya *doin'?
TIM: I'm *writin' it down.

TRACK 7A

Listen to the entire conversation again, spoken with relaxed (fast) pronunciation.

TRACK 7B

What Are You Doing This Weekend? **19**

COMPREHENSION

Answer these questions about the conversation.

1. What does Kenji want to do?
2. Does Tim want to do this? Explain.
3. Do you think Tim has ever gone bungee jumping? Explain.
4. What food does Kenji suggest?
5. Do you think this food is a good choice for bungee jumping? Explain.

Now, work with a partner and compare your answers.

PRACTICE

Close your book. You'll hear each part of the conversation spoken with relaxed pronunciation. Repeat each part using careful pronunciation.

TRACK 7C

Part 2 EXPANSION

COMPREHENSION

Listen to the conversation. The speakers use relaxed pronunciation. Answer the questions.

1. What's Kenji's advice about food and drink before the jump?
2. Why do you think Kenji gives this advice?
3. Who wants to jump first? Explain.
4. Why do you think Tim's writing a "will"?

Work with a partner. Compare your answers. Listen again if necessary.

TRACK 7D

20 Chapter 7

PRACTICE

Listen again. The conversation is spoken with relaxed pronunciation. Complete the sentences with the words you would hear if they were spoken with careful pronunciation. Then, listen once more and check your answers.

TRACK 7E

KENJI: So, ___(1)___ ___(2)___ ___(3)___ think we should do first?

TIM: ___(4)___ ___(5)___ ___(6)___ say to ___(7)___ some lunch? Should we eat before we bungee jump?

KENJI: No, that's not a good idea. Tim, ___(8)___ ___(9)___ ___(10)___ ___(11)___?

TIM: Soda.

KENJI: Water is better.

TIM: I drank all ___(12)___ my water. Could I have some ___(13)___ ___(14)___?

KENJI: Sure, but don't drink too much before ___(15)___ jump. Now, let's get ready.

TIM: ___(16)___ ___(17)___ we need to do?

KENJI: Decide who's ___(18)___ first. *You* look ready.

TIM: ___(19)___ ___(20)___ ___(21)___ mean? *I'm* not ready.

KENJI: Tim, ___(22)___ ___(23)___ ___(24)___ ___(25)___?

TIM: My "will."

DISCUSSION

Work in small groups.

What's the most exciting outdoor activity you like or would like to do? Explain.

What Are You Doing This Weekend? **21**

8 I Want to Have a Hamburger

want to ➡ *wanna

Part 1 INTRODUCTION

CONVERSATION

Listen to each part of the conversation: first spoken with careful (slow) pronunciation, then spoken with relaxed (fast) pronunciation.

Careful (Slow) Pronunciation	Relaxed (Fast) Pronunciation

JACK: What do you want to do?
KAREN: I'm starving. I want to eat out.
JACK: Okay. Where do you want to eat?
KAREN: I'm not sure. I don't want to spend a lot of money.
JACK: Hmm. Do you want to try Tom's Burgers?
KAREN: Maybe. Do they have low-fat lunches?
JACK: Sure. What do you want to have?
KAREN: I want to see the menu first.
JACK: When do you want to go there?
KAREN: I'm really hungry. I want to go there right now.

JACK: *Whaddaya *wanna do?
KAREN: I'm *starvin'. I *wanna eat out.
JACK: Okay. Where do *ya *wanna eat?
KAREN: I'm not sure. I don't *wanna spend a lot *a money.
JACK: Hmm. Do *ya *wanna try Tom's Burgers?
KAREN: Maybe. Do they have low-fat lunches?
JACK: Sure. *Whaddaya *wanna have?
KAREN: I *wanna see the menu first.
JACK: When do *ya *wanna go there?
KAREN: I'm really hungry. I *wanna go there right now.

TRACK 8A

Listen to the entire conversation again, spoken with relaxed (fast) pronunciation.

TRACK 8B

22 Chapter 8

COMPREHENSION

Answer these questions about the conversation.

1. In choosing a restaurant, what's important to Karen?
2. What kind of place is Tom's?
3. What kinds of food do you think you would find there?
4. How much do you think this food would cost?
5. Has either Karen or Jack been to Tom's before? Explain.

Now, work with a partner and compare your answers.

PRACTICE

Close your book. You'll hear each part of the conversation spoken with relaxed pronunciation. Repeat each part using careful pronunciation.

TRACK 8C

Part 2 EXPANSION

COMPREHENSION

Listen to the conversation. The speakers use relaxed pronunciation. Answer the questions.

1. What do Jack and Karen order for lunch?
2. Whose lunch is better? Why?
3. What doesn't Karen want to have? What could be the reason?
4. Who should pay for the lunches?
5. What's another way to offer to pay for someone's lunch?
6. Choose a more nutritious lunch for Jack and Karen. Explain your choices.
7. What would you order if you were eating at Tom's Burgers?

Work with a partner. Compare your answers. Listen again if necessary.

TRACK 8D

I Want to Have a Hamburger 23

PRACTICE

Listen again. The conversation is spoken with relaxed pronunciation. Complete the sentences with the words you would hear if they were spoken with careful pronunciation. Then, listen once more and check your answers.

TRACK 8E

JACK: __(1)__ __(2)__ __(3)__ __(4)__ __(5)__ have?

KAREN: Let's see. I __(6)__ __(7)__ try a chicken sandwich.

JACK: I __(8)__ __(9)__ have a cheeseburger and some fries. __(10)__ __(11)__ __(12)__ __(13)__ __(14)__ drink?

KAREN: I don't __(15)__ __(16)__ have a lot __(17)__ sugar. I'll have a large apple juice.

JACK: I __(18)__ __(19)__ try a chocolate shake. I hear the shakes here are very good.

CLERK: Can I help __(20)__?

KAREN: We __(21)__ __(22)__ order a chicken sandwich, a cheeseburger, one order __(23)__ fries, a large apple juice, and a chocolate shake.

CLERK: That'll be $11.15.

JACK: Here __(24)__ are.

KAREN: (*to Jack*) No, no. I __(25)__ __(26)__ pay __(27)__ __(28)__ lunch. *You* paid __(29)__ *my* lunch last time.

JACK: But –

KAREN: No. I insist.

JACK: Thank you. That's really nice __(30)__ __(31)__.

KAREN: (*to the clerk*) Here _____ are. (*She pays the clerk.*)
                                32

CLERK: Thank _____ very much.
              33

KAREN: Thank *you*.

DISCUSSION
Work in small groups.

Make a list of everything you ate yesterday. How nutritious was this food? Discuss.

9 We're Going to See "The Monster that Ate Cleveland"

going to + verb ⟶ *gonna

The *gonna pronunciation isn't used when there's no verb following *to*. Example:

I'm *going to* a movie.

Part 1 INTRODUCTION

CONVERSATION

Listen to each part of the conversation: first spoken with careful (slow) pronunciation, then spoken with relaxed (fast) pronunciation.

TRACK 9A

Careful (Slow) Pronunciation	Relaxed (Fast) Pronunciation
LISA: Oh, are you going to pay our bills tonight?	LISA: Oh, are *ya *gonna pay our bills tonight?
ANN: I'm going to try.	ANN: I'm *gonna try.
LISA: Thanks. I want to handle our money soon, but I'm so busy. So, what are you going to pay first?	LISA: Thanks. I *wanna handle our money soon, but I'm so busy. So, *whaddaya *gonna pay first?
ANN: First? Well, we're not going to have enough money for this month's electric bill.	ANN: First? Well, we're not *gonna have enough money *fer this month's electric bill.
LISA: You're not going to pay this month's electric bill?	LISA: *Yer not *gonna pay this month's electric bill?
ANN: Oh, I'm going to pay it, but not right now.	ANN: Oh, I'm *gonna pay it, but not right now.
LISA: When are you going to pay it?	LISA: When are *ya *gonna pay it?
ANN: I'm going to pay it after I pay last month's water bill.	ANN: I'm *gonna pay it after I pay last month's water bill.
LISA: You haven't paid last month's water bill?	LISA: *Ya haven't paid last month's water bill?
ANN: No. I'm going to pay last month's rent first.	ANN: No. I'm *gonna pay last month's rent first.

Listen to the entire conversation again, spoken with relaxed (fast) pronunciation.

TRACK 9B

COMPREHENSION

Answer these questions about the conversation.

1. What do you think the relationship between Lisa and Ann is?
2. Why doesn't Lisa pay their bills?
3. Does Ann do a good job with their money? Explain.
4. Should Lisa let Ann pay their bills? Explain.
5. Did Lisa know about the problems with their bills? Explain.
6. What do you think Lisa will say next?

Now, work with a partner and compare your answers.

PRACTICE

Close your book. You'll hear each part of the conversation spoken with relaxed pronunciation. Repeat each part using careful pronunciation.

TRACK 9C

Part 2 EXPANSION

COMPREHENSION

Listen to the conversation. The speakers use relaxed pronunciation. Answer the questions.

1. How old do you think Linda and Lisa are? Why?
2. Is Lisa sad? Explain.
3. What kind of movie are Linda and her sister going to see?
4. Why do you think Lisa asks if it's a comedy?
5. Why does Lisa want Ann to come to the movie?

TRACK 9D

Work with a partner. Compare your answers. Listen again if necessary.

We're Going to See "The Monster that Ate Cleveland" **27**

PRACTICE

Listen again. The conversation is spoken with relaxed pronunciation. Complete the sentences with the words you would hear if they were spoken with careful pronunciation. Then, listen once more and check your answers.

TRACK 9E

LINDA: So Lisa, __(1)__ __(2)__ __(3)__ __(4)__ __(5)__ do tonight?

LISA: Nothing. I'm just __(6)__ __(7)__ stay home.

LINDA: __(8)__ sound like __(9)__ depressed. What's wrong?

LISA: Oh, I just have a couple __(10)__ problems with my roommate. It's nothing. Are *you* __(11)__ __(12)__ do anything tonight?

LINDA: My sister and I are __(13)__ to a movie. Do __(14)__ __(15)__ __(16)__ come with us?

LISA: Well, maybe I should. __(17)__ __(18)__ __(19)__ __(20)__ __(21)__ see?

LINDA: *The Monster that Ate Cleveland.*

LISA: Is that a comedy?

LINDA: No. It's a horror movie.

LISA: The monster ate all __(22)__ Cleveland? Wow! I don't __(23)__ __(24)__ miss that. How soon are __(25)__ __(26)__ __(27)__ __(28)__ __(29)__ leave?

LINDA: We're __(30)__ __(31)__ __(32)__ __(33)__ leave in about fifteen minutes. Does __(34)__ roommate __(35)__ __(36)__ come with us?

LISA: Ann? That's a good idea. Maybe we'll be able to talk about our problems after the movie.

DISCUSSION

Work in small groups.

What's your favorite movie? Why?

28 Chapter 9

10 Can You See the Stage?

> can ➡ *kin
>
> can't ➡ can't (no change)
>
> Many learners have difficulty hearing the difference between *"can"* and *"can't."* *"Can"* reduces to *kin at a natural speed. In contrast, *"can't"* doesn't change pronunciation when said fast.

Part 1 INTRODUCTION

CONVERSATION

Listen to each part of the conversation: first spoken with careful (slow) pronunciation, then spoken with relaxed (fast) pronunciation.

TRACK 10A

Careful (Slow) Pronunciation	Relaxed (Fast) Pronunciation
CARLOS: I'm going to take a singing class. Do you want to take it with me?	CARLOS: I'm *gonna take a singing class. Do *ya *wanna take it with me?
TINA: I don't need a class. I can sing. My mother says I sound great.	TINA: I don't need a class. I *kin sing. My mother says I sound great.
CARLOS: Really? I want to hear you.	CARLOS: Really? I *wanna hear *ya.
TINA: I can't sing *now*.	TINA: I can't sing *now*.
CARLOS: Can't you just sing a few notes?	CARLOS: Can't *ya just sing a few notes?
TINA: All right. *I'm going to love you for the rest of my life. You're my beautiful stranger.*	TINA: All right. *I'm *gonna love *ya *fer the rest *a my life. *Yer my beautiful stranger.*
CARLOS: You can't sing.	CARLOS: *Ya can't sing.
TINA: What do you mean I can't sing? I sing with the car radio every day. I can sing.	TINA: *Whaddaya mean I can't sing? I sing with the car radio every day. I *kin sing.
CARLOS: I'm sorry. You're right. You sound really great. Can you write songs, too?	CARLOS: I'm sorry. *Yer right. *Ya sound really great. *Kin *ya write songs, too?
TINA: No. I can sing, but I can't write songs.	TINA: No. I *kin sing, but I can't write songs.

Listen to the entire conversation again, spoken with relaxed (fast) pronunciation.

TRACK 10B

COMPREHENSION

Answer these questions about the conversation.

1. Can Tina sing? Explain.
2. Why do you think Tina insists she can sing?
3. Why do you think Carlos says that she can't sing?
4. Why does Carlos apologize to Tina?
5. What are other ways for Carlos to apologize?

Now, work with a partner and compare your answers.

PRACTICE

Close your book. You'll hear each part of the conversation spoken with relaxed pronunciation. Repeat each part using careful pronunciation.

TRACK 10C

Part 2 EXPANSION

COMPREHENSION

Listen to the conversation. The speakers use relaxed pronunciation. Answer the questions.

1. What do you think the relationship between Carlos and Tina is? Explain.
2. Where are they?
3. Why can't they hear each other?
4. What kind of music do you think they're listening to? Explain.
5. What does Tina need Carlos to do with her popcorn? Why?
6. What does Carlos think she needs? Why?

TRACK 10D

Work with a partner. Compare your answers. Listen again if necessary.

30 Chapter 10

PRACTICE

Listen again. The conversation is spoken with relaxed pronunciation. Complete the sentences with the words you would hear if they were spoken with careful pronunciation. Then, listen once more and check your answers.

TRACK 10E

CARLOS: ___(1)___ ___(2)___ see the stage, Tina?

TINA: No. I ___(3)___ see over the head ___(4)___ the man in front ___(5)___ me. ___(6)___ ___(7)___ change seats with me?

CARLOS: Sure. ___(8)___ ___(9)___ see better now?

TINA: Yes. Thanks. Look! The band's ___(10)___ ___(11)___ start ___(12)___.

CARLOS: Aren't they great? Do ___(13)___ like the music?

TINA: ___(14)___ ___(15)___ ___(16)___ ___(17)___ ? I ___(18)___ hear ___(19)___ . ___(20)___ ___(21)___ speak up?

CARLOS: Are ___(22)___ ___(23)___ the music?

TINA: ___(24)___ ___(25)___ speak up? The Raging Onions are ___(26)___ so loudly, we ___(27)___ hear each other!

CARLOS: Do ___(28)___ like the music? I ___(29)___ talk any louder!

TINA: I love the music! I ___(30)___ ___(31)___ take a picture, but I ___(32)___ hold the popcorn at the same time. ___(33)___ ___(34)___ hold my popcorn ___(35)___ a minute?

CARLOS: Sure. I ___(36)___ get ___(37)___ more popcorn.

DISCUSSION

Work in small groups.

Who's your favorite singer? Why?

11 What Can I Get You for Your Cold?

get ⟶ *git

Part 1 INTRODUCTION

CONVERSATION

Listen to each part of the conversation: first spoken with careful (slow) pronunciation, then spoken with relaxed (fast) pronunciation.

Careful (Slow) Pronunciation

JEAN: Can I get you some chicken soup, honey?
NICK: No, I don't want to eat anything. My stomach's really hurting.
JEAN: Okay, but I'm going to get you some juice. You need liquids for your cough.
NICK: Can you get me some apple juice?
JEAN: Okay.
NICK: Oh, get me a straw, too.
JEAN: Sure.
NICK: Can I get up now, Mom?
JEAN: You can't get up until your fever goes away, honey.
NICK: Then, Mom, can you get me something to do? I'm *really* bored.

Relaxed (Fast) Pronunciation

JEAN: *Kin I *git *ya some chicken soup, honey?
NICK: No, I don't *wanna eat anything. My stomach's really *hurtin'.
JEAN: Okay, but I'm *gonna *git *ya some juice. *Ya need liquids *fer *yer cough.
NICK: *Kin *ya *git me some apple juice?
JEAN: Okay.
NICK: Oh, *git me a straw, too.
JEAN: Sure.
NICK: *Kin I *git up now, Mom?
JEAN: *Ya can't *git up until *yer fever goes away, honey.
NICK: Then, Mom, *kin *ya *git me something to do? I'm *really* bored.

TRACK 11A

Listen to the entire conversation again, spoken with relaxed (fast) pronunciation.

TRACK 11B

COMPREHENSION

Answer these questions about the conversation.

1. What's the relationship between Jean and Nick?
2. How old do you think Nick is? Explain.
3. Who can you call "honey"?
4. What are Nick's symptoms?
5. Why do you think Nick is bored?

Now, work with a partner and compare your answers.

PRACTICE

Close your book. You'll hear each part of the conversation spoken with relaxed pronunciation. Repeat each part using careful pronunciation.

TRACK 11C

Part 2 EXPANSION

COMPREHENSION

Listen to the conversation. The speakers use relaxed pronunciation. Answer the questions.

1. What's the relationship between Jean and Andrea?
2. Do you think it's a good relationship? Explain.
3. Who is sick?
4. What medicines does Jean need?
5. What's each medicine for?
6. Why do you think Jean needs sleep?

Work with a partner. Compare your answers. Listen again if necessary.

TRACK 11D

What Can I Get You for Your Cold? **33**

PRACTICE

Listen again. The conversation is spoken with relaxed pronunciation. Complete the sentences with the words you would hear if they were spoken with careful pronunciation. Then, listen once more and check your answers.

TRACK 11E

ANDREA: Hi, Jean.

JEAN: Hi, Andrea. Come in.

ANDREA: How are ___(1)___ ___(2)___?

JEAN: I'm fine, but Nick's still sick.

ANDREA: Oh? That's too bad. Kids ___(3)___ sick a lot. ___(4)___ I ___(5)___ ___(6)___ anything at the pharmacy? I'm ___(7)___ ___(8)___ go there, anyway.

JEAN: You are? Thanks so much. ___(9)___ a great sister.

ANDREA: No problem. You'd do the same ___(10)___ me. So, ___(11)___ ___(12)___ ___(13)___ need?

JEAN: ___(14)___ ___(15)___ ___(16)___ some children's cough syrup? Oh! And ___(17)___ ___(18)___ ___(19)___ me some antacid ___(20)___ Nick's stomach?

ANDREA: I'd better ___(21)___ some Tylenol, too. I borrowed ___(22)___ ___(23)___ my kids last week, remember? It's at my house.

JEAN: Oh, okay. Great. I guess that's it.

ANDREA: Not quite. What ___(24)___ I ___(25)___ ___(26)___ ___(27)___ *your* cough?

JEAN: What cough?

ANDREA: That cough. What ___(28)___ I ___(29)___ ___(30)___?

JEAN: ___(31)___ ___(32)___ ___(33)___ me some sleep? That's what I really need!

DISCUSSION

Work in small groups.

What do you do for a cold? What medicines do you take? What foods do you eat?

34 Chapter 11

12 Take Bus 4 to Second Street

to ⟶ *ta

To isn't pronounced **ta* if it's stressed or if it's not followed by another word. Example: Who do I give it *to*?

Part 1 INTRODUCTION

CONVERSATION

Listen to each part of the conversation: first spoken with careful (slow) pronunciation, then spoken with relaxed (fast) pronunciation.

TRACK 12A

Careful (Slow) Pronunciation	Relaxed (Fast) Pronunciation

KATHY: Excuse me. I'm going to the mall. What bus do I take?
MAN: Take Bus 4 to Second Street. Then you need to transfer to another bus.
KATHY: What bus do I need to transfer to?
MAN: You want to take Bus 89. It goes straight to the mall.
KATHY: Do I need to have exact change?
MAN: Yes. You need to put the exact change in the fare box on Bus 4.
KATHY: Do I need to pay again on Bus 89?
MAN: No. Ask the driver of Bus 4 to give you a transfer to Bus 89.
KATHY: What do you do with the transfer? Do you put it in the fare box?
MAN: No. You give it to the driver of Bus 89.

KATHY: Excuse me. I'm *goin' *ta the mall. What bus do I take?
MAN: Take Bus 4 *ta Second Street. Then *ya need *ta transfer *ta another bus.
KATHY: What bus do I need *ta transfer to?
MAN: *Ya *wanna take Bus 89. It goes straight *ta the mall.
Kathy: Do I need *ta have exact change?
MAN: Yes. *Ya need *ta put the exact change in the fare box on Bus 4.
KATHY: Do I need *ta pay again on Bus 89?
MAN: No. Ask the driver *a Bus 4 *ta give *ya a transfer *ta Bus 89.
KATHY: *Whaddaya do with the transfer? Do *ya put it in the fare box?
MAN: No. *Ya give it *ta the driver *a Bus 89.

Listen to the entire conversation again, spoken with relaxed (fast) pronunciation.

TRACK 12B

COMPREHENSION

Answer these questions about the conversation.

1. Where's Kathy going?
2. Do you think she often goes there by bus? Explain.
3. Which buses does she have to take to get there?
4. What does she need to do with the exact change for the fare?
5. How many times does she have to pay the fare? Explain.

Now, work with a partner and compare your answers.

PRACTICE

Close your book. You'll hear each part of the conversation spoken with relaxed pronunciation. Repeat each part using careful pronunciation.

TRACK 12C

Part 2 EXPANSION

COMPREHENSION

Listen to the conversation. The speakers use relaxed pronunciation. Answer the questions.

1. Why does Kathy say, "Excuse me"?
2. What do you think are other situations where you use "excuse me"?
3. What does Kathy need?
4. What's her "problem"?
5. How does the woman respond to Kathy's problem?

Work with a partner. Compare your answers. Listen again if necessary.

TRACK 12D

PRACTICE

Listen again. The conversation is spoken with relaxed pronunciation. Complete the sentences with the words you would hear if they were spoken with careful pronunciation. Then, listen once more and check your answers.

TRACK 12E

KATHY: Excuse me. Is this Bus 89?

WOMAN AT THE BUS STOP: Yes. Where do ____(1)____ need ____(2)____ go?

KATHY: ____(3)____ the mall. Is it far?

WOMAN: The Nature Mall?

KATHY: Yes.

WOMAN: I work part time at the mall. It's not far. I'll tell ____(4)____ when ____(5)____ ____(6)____ off.

KATHY: Thanks. That's really nice. ____(7)____ ____(8)____ answer a question ____(9)____ me?

WOMAN: Sure. ____(10)____ ____(11)____ ____(12)____ ____(13)____ ____(14)____ know?

KATHY: ____(15)____ ____(16)____ ____(17)____ think is the best place ____(18)____ shop at the mall?

WOMAN: Well, it depends. ____(19)____ ____(20)____ ____(21)____ ____(22)____ ____(23)____ ____(24)____ ____(25)____ buy?

KATHY: I need ____(26)____ ____(27)____ some shoes. But my feet are a little big. I need ____(28)____ find one ____(29)____ those large-size shoe stores.

WOMAN: ____(30)____ feet don't look big. They look fine.

KATHY: Thanks. That's nice ____(31)____ hear. I need ____(32)____ find some casual shoes. I also need ____(33)____ ____(34)____ some dress shoes.

WOMAN: Well, there are plenty ____(35)____ places ____(36)____ shop. I'm sure you'll be able ____(37)____ find some nice shoes.

DISCUSSION

Work in small groups.

What's the best kind of transportation you've ever used? Why?

13 I'm Going to Try to Find a Job

to after a vowel sound ⟶ **da*

The reduced form **da* is common after *go*.
To isn't pronounced **da* if stressed or if it's not followed by another word. Example:

A: **Kin *ya* fix this?

B: There's no way *to*.

Part 1 INTRODUCTION

CONVERSATION

Listen to each part of the conversation: first spoken with careful (slow) pronunciation, then spoken with relaxed (fast) pronunciation.

Careful (Slow) Pronunciation	Relaxed (Fast) Pronunciation

BILL: I want to go to Spain.
DAD: You want to go to Spain?
BILL: Yes.
DAD: Why do you want to go to Spain?
BILL: I want to try to learn about other cultures.
DAD: That's a really good idea, but who's going to pay for your trip?
BILL: Well, *you* are.
DAD: You want *me* to pay for it?
BILL: Well, I already tried to get the money from Mom.
DAD: I know a better way to get the money. Try to find a job.

BILL: I *wanna go *da Spain.
DAD: *Ya *wanna go *da Spain?
BILL: Yes.
DAD: Why do *ya *wanna go *da Spain?
BILL: I *wanna try *da learn about other cultures.
DAD: That's a really good idea, but who's *gonna pay *fer *yer trip?
BILL: Well, *you* are.
DAD: *Ya want *me *da pay *fer it?
BILL: Well, I already tried *ta *git the money from Mom.
DAD: I know a better way *da *git the money. Try *da find a job.

TRACK 13A

Listen to the entire conversation again, spoken with relaxed (fast) pronunciation.

TRACK 13B

38   Chapter 13

COMPREHENSION

Answer these questions about the conversation.

1. What does Bill want to do? Why?
2. How old do you think he is? Explain.
3. What's Bill's problem?
4. How does he try to solve his problem?
5. What's his father's solution to the problem?
6. Do you think this is a good solution? Explain.

Now, work with a partner and compare your answers.

PRACTICE

Close your book. You'll hear each part of the conversation spoken with relaxed pronunciation. Repeat each part using careful pronunciation.

TRACK 13C

Part 2 EXPANSION

COMPREHENSION

Listen to the conversation. The speakers use relaxed pronunciation. Answer the questions.

1. Where do you think Bill and Mohammed are? Explain.
2. What does Bill want? Why?
3. What do you think are other ways to find what Bill wants?
4. How does Bill look for a job on the Internet?
5. Is a dog trainer a job in the movie industry? Explain.
6. Do you think Bill wants this job? Explain.

TRACK 13D

Work with a partner. Compare your answers. Listen again if necessary.

I'm Going to Try to Find a Job   39

PRACTICE

Listen again. The conversation is spoken with relaxed pronunciation. Complete the sentences with the words you would hear if they were spoken with careful pronunciation. Then, listen once more and check your answers.

TRACK 13E

BILL: I need ___₁___ try ___₂___ find a job.

MOHAMMED: Why, Bill?

BILL: Because I ___₃___ ___₄___ ___₅___ ___₆___ Spain. It costs a lot ___₇___ money ___₈___ go there.

MOHAMMED: So, ask ___₉___ dad.

BILL: I did. He wants *me* ___₁₀___ pay ___₁₁___ the trip.

MOHAMMED: Oh. well, do ___₁₂___ ___₁₃___ ___₁₄___ try ___₁₅___ find a job on the Internet?

BILL: I don't know how ___₁₆___ do that. ___₁₇___ ___₁₈___ help me?

MOHAMMED: Sure. It's easy. First, go ___₁₉___ the Internet. Type the word "job." Then choose the kind ___₂₀___ jobs ___₂₁___ ___₂₂___ ___₂₃___ try ___₂₄___ find – education, health care, business...

BILL: Could I try ___₂₅___ find something in the movie industry?

MOHAMMED: Sure.

BILL: Okay. I did it.

MOHAMMED: Now choose the city ___₂₆___ ___₂₇___ ___₂₈___ work in. See? It's really easy ___₂₉___ do. There's the first one!

BILL: Dog trainer? Maybe I should look ___₃₀___ something in sales.

DISCUSSION

Work in small groups.

When is someone old enough to get a job? Explain.

14 I've Got to Check Your Teeth

got to → *gotta
have to → *hafta
has to → *hasta

Part 1 INTRODUCTION

CONVERSATION

Listen to each part of the conversation: first spoken with careful (slow) pronunciation, then spoken with relaxed (fast) pronunciation.

Careful (Slow) Pronunciation

JOE: My tooth's driving me crazy.
GEORGE: Then you've got to make an appointment with a dentist.
JOE: I've got to find one first. I don't have a dentist.
GEORGE: I have to go downtown. Come on. Let's go to *my* dentist.
JOE: I can't. I have to study.
GEORGE: Are you going to go to the dentist after that? Your tooth has to be taken care of.
JOE: I know it has to be taken care of. But I've got to get some gas.
GEORGE: *Then* are you going to go to the dentist?
JOE: Well, no. After that, I have to go to the bank.
GEORGE: Okay, but after you go to the bank, you've got to go to the dentist!

Relaxed (Fast) Pronunciation

JOE: My tooth's *drivin' me crazy.
GEORGE: Then you've *gotta make an appointment with a dentist.
JOE: I've *gotta find one first. I don't have a dentist.
GEORGE: I *hafta go downtown. Come on. Let's go *da my dentist.
JOE: I can't. I *hafta study.
GEORGE: Are *ya *gonna go *da the dentist after that? *Yer tooth *hasta be taken care of.
JOE: I know it *hasta be taken care of. But I've *gotta *git some gas.
GEORGE: *Then* are *ya *gonna go *da the dentist?
JOE: Well, no. After that, I *hafta go *da the bank.
GEORGE: Okay, but after *ya go *da the bank, you've *gotta go *da the dentist!

TRACK 14A

Listen to the entire conversation again, spoken with relaxed (fast) pronunciation.

TRACK 14B

COMPREHENSION

Answer these questions about the conversation.

1. What's Joe's problem?
2. Why can't Joe make an appointment with a dentist?
3. Do you think Joe is really too busy to see the dentist? Explain.
4. Do you think Joe visits the dentist often? Explain.

Now, work with a partner and compare your answers.

PRACTICE

Close your book. You'll hear each part of the conversation spoken with relaxed pronunciation. Repeat each part using careful pronunciation.

TRACK 14C

Part 2 EXPANSION

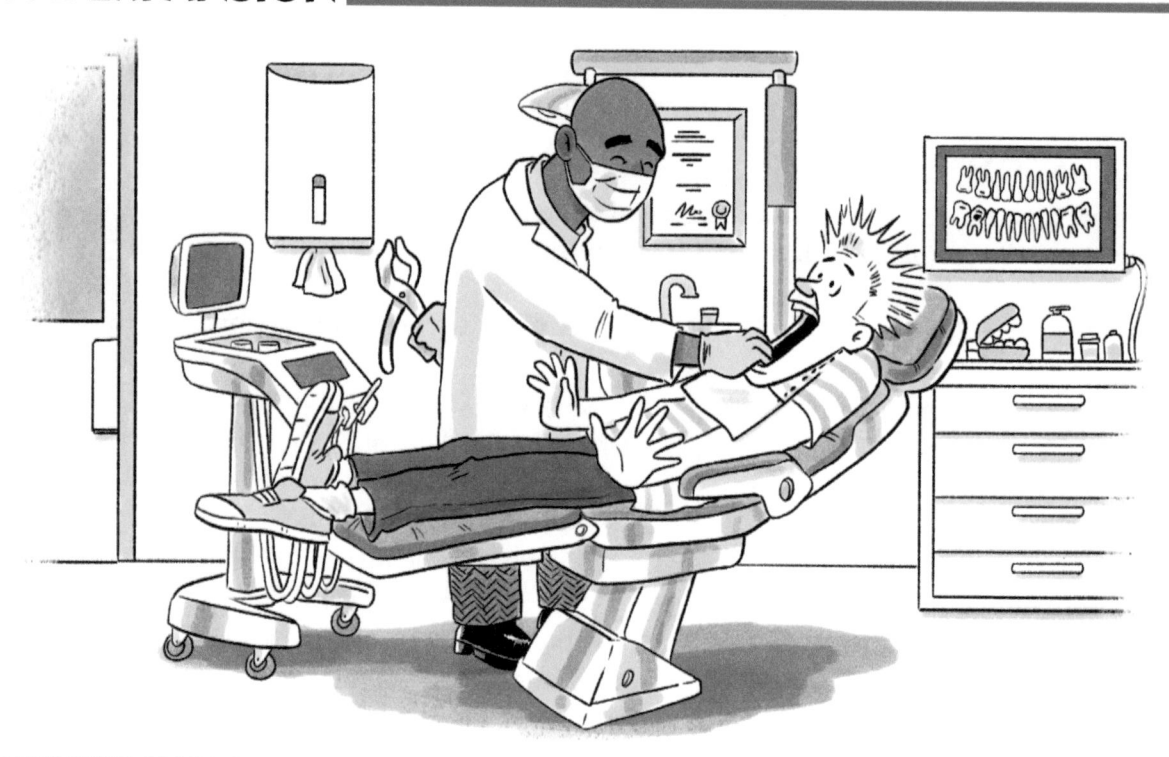

COMPREHENSION

Listen to the conversation. The speakers use relaxed pronunciation. Answer the questions.

1. What's Joe worried about?
2. What did the dentist do?
3. What's the dentist going to do tomorrow?
4. How often do you think Joe should see the dentist? Why?

TRACK 14D

Work with a partner. Compare your answers. Listen again if necessary.

42   Chapter 13

PRACTICE

Listen again. The conversation is spoken with relaxed pronunciation. Complete the sentences with the words you would hear if they were spoken with careful pronunciation. Then, listen once more and check your answers.

TRACK 14E

JOE: The dentist has __(1)__ __(2)__ see me soon. My tooth really hurts! He __(3)__ __(4)__ do something about it.

GEORGE: Don't worry, Joe. I'm sure the dentist is __(5)__ __(6)__ be able __(7)__ help __(8)__. __(9)__ won't __(10)__ __(11)__ wait very long.

JOE: __(12)__ don't think the dentist is __(13)__ __(14)__ tell me he __(15)__ __(16)__ pull my tooth, do __(17)__?

GEORGE: I'm not sure. If the dentist __(18)__ __(19)__ pull it, he will, but I'm sure he'll try __(20)__ save it if he __(21)__.

JOE: Well, I guess I won't __(22)__ __(23)__ wait any longer __(24)__ find out. He's ready __(25)__ see me now.

(Later)

GEORGE: What happened?

JOE: Well, first he said he'd __(26)__ __(27)__ check the tooth.

GEORGE: Then what happened? Did he __(28)__ __(29)__ pull it?

JOE: No. He decided __(30)__ fill it, not pull it. But he said I've __(31)__ __(32)__ come back tomorrow. He's __(33)__ __(34)__ take some x-rays, and he __(35)__ __(36)__ check my other teeth.

GEORGE: You've __(37)__ __(38)__ see the dentist more often!

DISCUSSION

Work in small groups.

Do your family and friends go to the dentist regularly?
How often do you go to the dentist? How often should you go? Discuss.

I've Got to Check Your Teeth

15 She Used to Ride a Harley

used to ⟶ *useta

supposed to ⟶ *supposta

Part 1 INTRODUCTION

CONVERSATION

Listen to each part of the conversation: first spoken with careful (slow) pronunciation, then spoken with relaxed (fast) pronunciation.

Careful (Slow) Pronunciation

HENRY: Is my breakfast ready yet? I want to go to the park.
OLGA: Not yet. You know, before he died, my first husband used to cook breakfast for me every Sunday.
HENRY: Manuel used to cook for *you*? Men aren't supposed to cook.
OLGA: What do you mean, men aren't supposed to cook?
HENRY: Women are supposed to cook.
OLGA: He used to sew curtains for us, too.
HENRY: You're kidding, right? Men aren't supposed to sew. Before my first wife died, she used to always say–
OLGA: Nina used to ride a Harley-Davidson motorcycle to work, didn't she?
HENRY: Well, yes, but she used to ride it *after* she made my breakfast.

Relaxed (Fast) Pronunciation

HENRY: Is my breakfast ready yet? I *wanna go *da the park.
OLGA: Not yet. *Ya know, before he died, my first husband *useta cook breakfast *fer me every Sunday.
HENRY: Manuel *useta cook *fer *you*? Men aren't *supposta cook.
OLGA: *Whaddaya mean, men aren't *supposta cook?
HENRY: Women are *supposta cook.
OLGA: He *useta sew curtains *fer us, too.
HENRY: *Yer *kiddin', right? Men aren't *supposta sew. Before my first wife died, she *useta always say–
OLGA: Nina *useta ride a Harley-Davidson motorcycle *ta work, didn't she?
HENRY: Well, yes, but she *useta ride it *after* she made my breakfast.

TRACK 15A

Listen to the entire conversation again, spoken with relaxed (fast) pronunciation.

TRACK 15B

COMPREHENSION

Answer these questions about the conversation.

1. What do you think the relationship between Henry and Olga is?
2. What does Henry think a woman should do?
3. What does Olga think a man should do?
4. Have Henry and Olga been married before? Explain.
5. What do you know about Olga's first husband?
6. What do you know about Henry's first wife?

Now, work with a partner and compare your answers.

PRACTICE

Close your book. You'll hear each part of the conversation spoken with relaxed pronunciation. Repeat each part using careful pronunciation.

TRACK 15C

Part 2 EXPANSION

COMPREHENSION

Listen to the conversation. The speakers use relaxed pronunciation. Answer the questions.

1. Where do you think Henry and Jack are?
2. How old do you think they are? Explain.
3. In what ways is the world changing too fast for them?
4. Do you think they know each other well? Why or why not?
5. What do you know about Henry?
6. What do you know about Jack?

Work with a partner. Compare your answers. Listen again if necessary.

TRACK 15D

She Used to Ride a Harley **45**

PRACTICE

Listen again. The conversation is spoken with relaxed pronunciation. Complete the sentences with the words you would hear if they were spoken with careful pronunciation. Then, listen once more and check your answers.

TRACK 15E

HENRY: ___(1)___ ___(2)___ ask ___(3)___ a better day than today.

JACK: No. ___(4)___ ___(5)___.

HENRY: I was ___(6)___ ___(7)___ stay home and cook breakfast this morning. My wife doesn't ___(8)___ ___(9)___ cook breakfast on Sundays. But it's too nice a day ___(10)___ stay home.

JACK: ___(11)___ right. It's a beautiful day. ___(12)___ not ___(13)___ ___(14)___ stay inside on a day like today.

HENRY: I completely agree. ___(15)___ know, I ___(16)___ ___(17)___ go ___(18)___ the park on Seventh Avenue. Do ___(19)___ remember that park? They tore it down ___(20)___ build a shopping mall.

JACK: Yeah. That was terrible. I ___(21)___ ___(22)___ go there after work.

HENRY: Aren't we ___(23)___ ___(24)___ care more about parks than buildings?

JACK: We're ___(25)___ ___(26)___. Yeah. The world's ___(27)___ too fast ___(28)___ me.

HENRY: Me, too. By the way, my name's Henry.

JACK: Nice ___(29)___ meet ___(30)___, Henry. My name's Jack.

HENRY: So, Jack, what kind ___(31)___ work did ___(32)___ do?

JACK: I ___(33)___ ___(34)___ be a farmer. I raised wheat.

HENRY: Oh? I ___(35)___ ___(36)___ be an engineer ___(37)___ the railroad. I was an engineer ___(38)___ fifty years.

JACK: I ___(39)___ ___(40)___ be married ___(41)___ a wonderful woman.

46   Chapter 15

HENRY: Was she a good cook?

JACK: Oh, yeah. She _____ _____ cook wonderful meals.
                    42   43

HENRY: Wives are _____ _____ cook _____
                   44   45   46
their husbands, aren't they?

JACK: Oh, yeah. Definitely. They're _____ _____ cook,
                                      47   48
clean, sew, all _____ that stuff.
                    49

HENRY: That's not an old-fashioned idea, is it?

JACK: Not _____ me.
            50

DISCUSSION
Work in small groups.

Should a man cook, sew, or clean the house? Should a woman make money, fix a car, or ride a motorcycle? Explain.

16 What's the Fastest Way to Send His Packages?

he	→ *'e
his	→ *'is
him	→ *'im
her	→ *'er
them	→ *'em

These pronunciations are not used when *he*, *his*, *him*, *her*, and *them* are stressed.

Part 1 INTRODUCTION

CONVERSATION

Listen to each part of the conversation: first spoken with careful (slow) pronunciation, then spoken with relaxed (fast) pronunciation.

Careful (Slow) Pronunciation

MICHIKO: Can you help me?
PAULA: Sure. What do you need?
MICHIKO: Well, I'm going to mail these packages to my parents. I want them to get them as soon as possible.
PAULA: How fast do you want them to get them?
MICHIKO: Faster than my brother got the package I sent *him*.
PAULA: When did he get it?
MICHIKO: Well, I sent him the package last month. Do you know when he got it? Last week!
PAULA: How did you send it?
MICHIKO: I sent his package first class.
PAULA: Wow. I sent my sister a package, and it only took her four days to get it.

Relaxed (Fast) Pronunciation

MICHIKO: *Kin *ya help me?
PAULA: Sure. *Whaddaya need?
MICHIKO: Well, I'm *gonna mail these packages *ta my parents. I want *'em *ta *git *'em as soon as possible.
PAULA: How fast do *ya want *'em *ta *git *'em?
MICHIKO: Faster than my brother got the package I sent *him*.
PAULA: When did *'e *git it?
MICHIKO: Well, I sent *'im the package last month. Do *ya know when *'e got it? Last week!
PAULA: How did *ya send it?
MICHIKO: I sent *'is package first class.
PAULA: Wow. I sent my sister a package, and it only took *'er four days *ta *git it.

TRACK 16A

Listen to the entire conversation again, spoken with relaxed (fast) pronunciation.

TRACK 16B

COMPREHENSION

Answer these questions about the conversation.

1. What's Michiko's problem?
2. Michiko says, "I want them to get them as soon as possible." Who or what is the first "them"? Who or what is the second "them"?
3. Why could Michiko's package have taken so long to get to her brother?
4. How do you think Paula sent the package to her sister?
5. Does Paula help Michiko with her problem? Explain.

Now, work with a partner and compare your answers.

PRACTICE

Close your book. You'll hear each part of the conversation spoken with relaxed pronunciation. Repeat each part using careful pronunciation.

TRACK 16C

Part 2 EXPANSION

COMPREHENSION

Listen to the conversation. The speakers use relaxed pronunciation. Answer the questions.

1. Where are Michiko and the clerk?
2. Why does the clerk want to talk to his supervisor?
3. What are the two best ways to send Michiko's packages?
4. Which packages have to arrive first – her parents' or her uncle's? Explain.
5. Why do you think the packages to Michiko's uncle have to arrive by Friday?

TRACK 16D

Work with a partner. Compare your answers. Listen again if necessary.

What's the Fastest Way to Send His Packages?

PRACTICE

Listen again. The conversation is spoken with relaxed pronunciation. Complete the sentences with the words you would hear if they were spoken with careful pronunciation. Then, listen once more and check your answers.

TRACK 16E

MICHIKO: Hi. I ___(1)___ ___(2)___ send these packages ___(3)___ New York.

CLERK: How do ___(4)___ ___(5)___ ___(6)___ send ___(7)___?

MICHIKO: I'm not sure. I'm ___(8)___ ___(9)___ ___(10)___ my uncle, and I ___(11)___ ___(12)___ ___(13)___ ___(14)___ to ___(15)___ by Friday. ___(16)___ ___(17)___ ___(18)___ suggest?

CLERK: I'm new here. I'll go talk ___(19)___ my supervisor. I'll ask ___(20)___ what the fastest way would be.

MICHIKO: Tell ___(21)___ that they ___(22)___ ___(23)___ ___(24)___ ___(25)___ my uncle as soon as possible, and that ___(26)___ ___(27)___ ___(28)___ ___(29)___ ___(30)___ no later than Friday.

CLERK: I'll tell ___(31)___.

(A few minutes later)

MICHIKO: What's ___(32)___ advice?

CLERK: She says ___(33)___ should send ___(34)___ to ___(35)___ by Priority Mail or Express Mail. Express Mail's the fastest, but it's expensive. If ___(36)___ send ___(37)___ ___(38)___ ___(39)___ uncle by Priority Mail, it's cheaper, but ___(40)___ might not ___(41)___ ___(42)___ ___(43)___ a few days.

MICHIKO: If I send ___(44)___ packages to ___(45)___ by Priority Mail, will ___(46)___ ___(47)___ ___(48)___ by Friday?

50   Chapter 16

CLERK: Maybe. If _____(49)_____ luck's good, _____(50)_____ will, but I _____(51)_____ promise anything.

MICHIKO: Then I'll send my uncle _____(52)_____ packages by Express Mail. I'm also _____(53)_____ _____(54)_____ send some packages _____(55)_____ my parents. I guess I'll send my parents' packages by Priority Mail. Thanks.

CLERK: _____(56)_____ welcome.

DISCUSSION
Work in small groups.

What's the worst experience you've ever had sending or receiving mail? Explain.

17 We Arrive on Tuesday and Leave on Thursday

and ⟶ *'n'

And isn't pronounced *'n' if stressed.

Part 1 INTRODUCTION

CONVERSATION

Listen to each part of the conversation: first spoken with careful (slow) pronunciation, then spoken with relaxed (fast) pronunciation.

Careful (Slow) Pronunciation	Relaxed (Fast) Pronunciation

JULIE: I want to make a reservation for Tuesday, April 6.
RESERVATIONS: We have a single room and a double room available for the 6th.
JULIE: Does the double have a refrigerator and an extra bed?
RESERVATIONS: It has a refrigerator, and we can get you a rollaway bed.
JULIE: Is it quiet? And is there a charge for children under three?
RESERVATIONS: Yes, it's very quiet, and there's no charge for children.
JULIE: Great. I'll take it. There'll be four people: myself, my husband, and two children.
RESERVATIONS: Fine. I'll need your name and a credit card number to hold that room.
JULIE: My name is Julie Kim, K-I-M, and my credit card number is 453…
RESERVATIONS: Excuse me. An airplane flew overhead, and I couldn't hear. What's your…

JULIE: I *wanna make a reservation *fer Tuesday, April 6.
RESERVATIONS: We have a single room *'n' a double room available *fer the 6th.
JULIE: Does the double have a refrigerator *'n' an extra bed?
RESERVATIONS: It has a refrigerator, *'n' we *kin *git *ya a rollaway bed.
JULIE: Is it quiet? *'N' is there a charge *fer children under three?
RESERVATIONS: Yes, it's very quiet, *'n' there's no charge *fer children.
JULIE: Great. I'll take it. There'll be four people: myself, my husband, *'n' two children.
RESERVATIONS: Fine. I'll need *yer name *'n' a credit card number *ta hold that room.
JULIE: My name is Julie Kim, K-I-M, *'n' my credit card number is 453…
RESERVATIONS: Excuse me. An airplane flew overhead, *'n' I couldn't hear. What's *yer…

TRACK 17A

Listen to the entire conversation again, spoken with relaxed (fast) pronunciation.

TRACK 17B

COMPREHENSION

Answer these questions about the conversation.

1. What does Julie want? When?
2. How old do you think Julie's children are? Explain.
3. What do you know about the room?
4. Why will Julie have to repeat her credit card number?
5. Do you think Julie will like the room? Explain.

Now, work with a partner and compare your answers.

PRACTICE

Close your book. You'll hear each part of the conversation spoken with relaxed pronunciation. Repeat each part using careful pronunciation.

TRACK 17C

Part 2 EXPANSION

COMPREHENSION

Listen to the conversation. The speakers use relaxed pronunciation. Answer the questions.

1. Where's Julie?
2. What's wrong with the room?
3. Why can't Julie order something from Room Service?
4. Do you think the front desk clerk is doing a good job? Explain.
5. Do you think Julie should complain to the manager about the hotel? Explain.

TRACK 17D

Work with a partner. Compare your answers. Listen again if necessary.

We Arrive on Tuesday and Leave on Thursday   53

PRACTICE

Listen again. The conversation is spoken with relaxed pronunciation. Complete the sentences with the words you would hear if they were spoken with careful pronunciation. Then, listen once more and check your answers.

TRACK 17E

JULIE: Excuse me. It's 10 P.M., _____(1) the man next door is _____(2) _____(3) _____(4) the guitar.

FRONT DESK: He's _____(5) _____(6) _____(7) the guitar?

JULIE: Yes. _____(8) _____(9) hear _____(10)?

FRONT DESK: I'll send somebody _____(11) talk _____(12) _____(13) right away.

JULIE: Thank you.

FRONT DESK: Excuse me. I _____(14) hear _____(15). There's an airplane–

JULIE: Thank you! _____(16) _____(17) we have a rollaway bed? The reservations clerk said you'd have a rollaway bed _____(18) me, _____(19) it's not here.

FRONT DESK: I'll check . . . Okay, we have a rollaway bed reserved _____(20) Room 27, _____(21) then _____(22) is right here. I'll send it up.

JULIE: _____(23) the refrigerator doesn't work. _____(24) we order some sandwiches _____(25) sodas from Room Service?

FRONT DESK: I'm sorry. Room Service closes at 10 P.M.

JULIE: We _____(26) order just one sandwich _____(27) a soda?

FRONT DESK: Excuse me. Another airplane just-

JULIE: _____(28) we order a sandwich _____(29) a soda?

FRONT DESK: I'm really sorry. There's a vending machine with chips _____30_____

candy at the end _____31_____ the hall.

JULIE: Chips _____32_____ candy? That's it?

FRONT DESK: Room Service opens at 8:00 A.M., _____33_____ _____34_____

_____35_____ order breakfast then. I'm really sorry.

JULIE: All right. Oh, _____36_____ one more question. Who _____37_____

I complain _____38_____ about this hotel?

DISCUSSION
Work in small groups.

Describe the best hotel or motel you've ever stayed at. Then describe the worst.

18 Do You Want a Chocolate or Lemon Birthday Cake?

or ⟶ *er

Or isn't pronounced *er if it's stressed.

Part 1 INTRODUCTION

CONVERSATION

Listen to each part of the conversation: first spoken with careful (slow) pronunciation, then spoken with relaxed (fast) pronunciation.

| Careful (Slow) Pronunciation | Relaxed (Fast) Pronunciation |

DAVID: So, do you want to have your birthday party at the park or a restaurant?
JAMIE: Both.
DAVID: Honey, you can't have both. The park or a restaurant?
JAMIE: I want to go to... the park.
DAVID: Okay. Do you want a chocolate or a lemon birthday cake?
JAMIE: Uh...both.
DAVID: Honey, you have to make a choice - chocolate or lemon?
JAMIE: Chocolate.
DAVID: Good. And which toy do you want to bring - the truck or the airplane?
JAMIE: I don't want to bring the truck *or* the airplane. I want to get a new toy.

DAVID: So, do *ya *wanna have *yer birthday party at the park *er a restaurant?
JAMIE: Both.
DAVID: Honey, *ya can't have both. The park *er a restaurant?
JAMIE: I *wanna go *da... the park.
DAVID: Okay. Do *ya want a chocolate *er a lemon birthday cake?
JAMIE: Uh...both.
DAVID: Honey, *ya *hafta make a choice - chocolate *er lemon?
JAMIE: Chocolate.
DAVID: Good. *'N' which toy do *ya *wanna bring - the truck *er the airplane?
JAMIE: I don't *wanna bring the truck *or* the airplane. I *wanna *git a new toy.

TRACK 18A

Listen to the entire conversation again, spoken with relaxed (fast) pronunciation.

TRACK 18B

COMPREHENSION

Answer these questions about the conversation.

1. What do you think the relationship between David and Jamie is?
2. What's David planning?
3. What decisions does Jamie have to make?
4. How old do you think Jamie is? Explain.
5. Why do you think Jamie wants to get a new toy?

Now, work with a partner and compare your answers.

PRACTICE

Close your book. You'll hear each part of the conversation spoken with relaxed pronunciation. Repeat each part using careful pronunciation.

TRACK 18C

Part 2 EXPANSION

COMPREHENSION

Listen to the conversation. The speakers use relaxed pronunciation. Answer the questions.

1. Where do you think David, Brenda, and Jamie are?
2. What do you think their relationship to each other is?
3. What are they celebrating?
4. What are all of the things they do to celebrate?
5. What's Jamie's wish?
6. Why shouldn't Jamie tell anybody the wish?

Work with a partner. Compare your answers. Listen again if necessary.

TRACK 18D

Do You Want a Chocolate or Lemon Birthday Cake? **57**

PRACTICE

Listen again. The conversation is spoken with relaxed pronunciation. Complete the sentences with the words you would hear if they were spoken with careful pronunciation. Then, listen once more and check your answers.

TRACK 18E

DAVID: So, Jamie, do ____(1)____ ____(2)____ ____(3)____ play on the swings first ____(4)____ do ____(5)____ ____(6)____ ____(7)____ eat?

JAMIE: I ____(8)____ ____(9)____ eat first.

BRENDA: Okay, honey. ____(10)____ ____(11)____ ____(12)____ want? A hot dog ____(13)____ a hamburger?

JAMIE: Both.

DAVID: Both? Where are ____(14)____ ____(15)____ ____(16)____ put all ____(17)____ that food?

JAMIE: It's my birthday. I've ____(18)____ ____(19)____ eat more now because I'm older.

BRENDA: I ____(20)____ argue with that. Do ____(21)____ want ketchup ____(22)____ mustard on ____(23)____ hot dog?

JAMIE: I want mustard. ____(24)____ I don't want anything on my hamburger.

BRENDA: Okay. Here ____(25)____ are.

(Ten minutes later)

BRENDA: ____(26)____ ____(27)____ ____(28)____ think, Jamie? Should we open ____(29)____ presents now ____(30)____ after we eat the cake?

JAMIE: After we eat the cake.

BRENDA: David, ____(31)____ ____(32)____ light the candles, ____(33)____ do ____(34)____ want me ____(35)____ do it?

DAVID: I'll do it.

BRENDA: Okay, Jamie, close ____(36)____ eyes, make a wish, ____(37)____ blow out the candles.

58 Chapter 18

DAVID: Wow! _____38_____ blew _____39_____ all out! Now _____40_____ _____41_____ _____42_____ wish.

JAMIE: _____43_____ mean, tomorrow I _____44_____ have another birthday party at a restaurant?

BRENDA: Honey, _____45_____ not _____46_____ _____47_____ tell us _____48_____ wish, _____49_____ it won't happen.

JAMIE: But, if I don't tell _____50_____ my wish, how _____51_____ _____52_____ give it _____53_____ me?

DISCUSSION
Work in small groups.

What do you do to celebrate your birthday? Explain.

19 I Don't Know What Classes to Take

don't know ⟶ *donno

Part 1 INTRODUCTION

CONVERSATION

Listen to each part of the conversation: first spoken with careful (slow) pronunciation, then spoken with relaxed (fast) pronunciation.

Careful (Slow) Pronunciation

TONY: I don't know what classes to take next semester.
LISA: Well, what are you thinking of taking?
TONY: I don't know. The problem is that I'm going to be working afternoons.
LISA: Are you going to be working all semester?
TONY: I don't know right now.
LISA: What do you want to do when you finish school?
TONY: That's another problem. I don't know.
LISA: Do you want to talk with a counselor?
TONY: I don't know. What do you think?
LISA: If you don't know what to do, you have to talk to somebody.

Relaxed (Fast) Pronunciation

TONY: I *donno what classes *ta take next semester.
LISA: Well, *whaddaya *thinkin' *a *takin'?
TONY: I *donno. The problem is that I'm *gonna be *workin' afternoons.
LISA: Are *ya *gonna be *workin' all semester?
TONY: I *donno right now.
LISA: *Whaddaya *wanna do when *ya finish school?
TONY: That's another problem. I *donno.
LISA: Do *ya *wanna talk with a counselor?
TONY: I *donno. *Whaddaya think?
LISA: If *ya *donno what *ta do, *ya *hafta talk *ta somebody.

TRACK 19A

Listen to the entire conversation again, spoken with relaxed (fast) pronunciation.

TRACK 19B

COMPREHENSION

Answer these questions about the conversation.

1. What's Tony's problem?
2. What do you think the relationship between Tony and Lisa is?
3. How old do you think Tony is? Explain.
4. Why do you think Lisa asks him what he wants to do after he finishes school?
5. What do you think Tony finally decides to do? Why?

Now, work with a partner and compare your answers.

PRACTICE

Close your book. You'll hear each part of the conversation spoken with relaxed pronunciation. Repeat each part using careful pronunciation.

TRACK 19C

Part 2 EXPANSION

COMPREHENSION

Listen to the conversation. The speakers use relaxed pronunciation. Answer the questions.

1. Why isn't Tony sure about taking engineering classes?
2. Do you think Tony has confidence in himself? Explain.
3. Do you think Tony really wants to be an engineer? Explain.
4. Do you think a lot of people have the same problem as Tony? Explain.
5. What would your advice to Tony be?

TRACK 19D

Work with a partner. Compare your answers. Listen again if necessary.

I Don't Know What Classes to Take **61**

PRACTICE

Listen again. The conversation is spoken with relaxed pronunciation. Complete the sentences with the words you would hear if they were spoken with careful pronunciation. Then, listen once more and check your answers.

TRACK 19E

COUNSELOR: So, Tony, how are ___(1)___ ___(2)___ today?

TONY: I ___(3)___ ___(4)___ .

COUNSELOR: Well, what ___(5)___ I help ___(6)___ with?

TONY: I ___(7)___ ___(8)___ what classes ___(9)___ take next semester.

COUNSELOR: ___(10)___ a freshman, right?

TONY: Yes.

COUNSELOR: Okay, ___(11)___ ___(12)___ ___(13)___ ___(14)___ ___(15)___ do after ___(16)___ graduate?

TONY: I ___(17)___ ___(18)___ .

COUNSELOR: There's nothing ___(19)___ ___(20)___ ___(21)___ do?

TONY: Well, my grandfather ___(22)___ ___(23)___ be an engineer. I'm ___(24)___ about studying engineering, but I ___(25)___ ___(26)___ if I'll do well.

COUNSELOR: We have some excellent engineering classes ___(27)___ ___(28)___ take. Have ___(29)___ talked ___(30)___ ___(31)___ parents about this, Tony?

TONY: No. They ___(32)___ ___(33)___ yet.

COUNSELOR: Well, if ___(34)___ really ___(35)___ about being an engineer, ___(36)___ ___(37)___ ___(38)___ at least try. Then if ___(39)___ don't like it, ___(40)___ ___(41)___ try something else.

TONY: All right. Do ___(42)___ have any engineering classes in the mornings?

COUNSELOR: I ___(43)___ ___(44)___ . I'll check.

DISCUSSION

Work in small groups.

What can people do to increase their confidence?

20 Can't You Find an Apartment?

/t/ + you → *cha

/t/ + your
/t/ + you're } → *cher

Part 1 INTRODUCTION

CONVERSATION

Listen to each part of the conversation: first spoken with careful (slow) pronunciation, then spoken with relaxed (fast) pronunciation.

Careful (Slow) Pronunciation

HIRO: Can't you find an apartment?
SAM: No, I can't. The rent you have to pay is too high.
HIRO: You know, I have a friend who could try to get you an apartment.
SAM: You do?
HIRO: Yeah. He used to be a real estate salesperson.
SAM: Well, I don't want your friend to spend a lot of time on it.
HIRO: No problem. I'll tell him that you're new in town.
SAM: Great. Thank him in advance for me, okay?
HIRO: Sure. Tell me what you're looking for. Do you want a furnished or unfurnished apartment?
SAM: I don't know. Don't you think a furnished apartment would be expensive?

Relaxed (Fast) Pronunciation

HIRO: Can't *cha find an apartment?
SAM: No, I can't. The rent *cha *hafta pay is too high.
HIRO: *Ya know, I have a friend who could try *da *git *cha an apartment.
SAM: *Ya do?
HIRO: Yeah. He *useta be a real estate salesperson.
SAM: Well, I don't want *cher friend *ta spend a lot *a time on it.
HIRO: No problem. I'll tell *'im that *cher new in town.
SAM: Great. Thank *'im in advance *fer me, okay?
HIRO: Sure. Tell me what *cher *lookin' for. Do *ya want a furnished *er unfurnished apartment?
SAM: I *donno. Don't *cha think a furnished apartment would be expensive?

TRACK 20A

TRACK 20B

Listen to the entire conversation again, spoken with relaxed (fast) pronunciation.

COMPREHENSION

Answer these questions about the conversation.

1. What does Sam want?
2. Why can't Sam find what he wants?
3. Is Hiro's friend still a real estate salesperson?
4. Do you think Hiro's friend can help Sam? Explain.

Now, work with a partner and compare your answers.

PRACTICE

Close your book. You'll hear each part of the conversation spoken with relaxed pronunciation. Repeat each part using careful pronunciation.

TRACK 20C

Part 2 EXPANSION

COMPREHENSION

Listen to the conversation. The speakers use relaxed pronunciation. Answer the questions.

1. How do the speakers introduce themselves?
2. What are other ways they could introduce themselves?
3. What are possible reasons that Sam doesn't want a roommate?
4. What does Mark know about Sam?
5. Do you think it will take a long time to find an apartment for Sam? Explain.
6. Do you think Sam has a job? Explain.

Work with a partner. Compare your answers. Listen again if necessary.

TRACK 20D

64 Chapter 20

PRACTICE

Listen again. The conversation is spoken with relaxed pronunciation. Complete the sentences with the words you would hear if they were spoken with careful pronunciation. Then, listen once more and check your answers.

TRACK 20E

SAM: Hi. I'm Sam Trump.

MARK: How are _____1_____? I'm Mark Baker.

SAM: Nice _____2_____ meet _____3_____.

MARK: Nice _____4_____ meet _____5_____, too.

SAM: My friend, Hiro, said that _____6_____ could help me. I _____7_____ _____8_____ find an apartment.

MARK: Sure. Hiro told me about _____9_____. Do _____10_____ know _____11_____ _____12_____ _____13_____ for?

SAM: A one-bedroom apartment, but it's _____14_____ _____15_____ be cheap.

MARK: Then why _____16_____ _____17_____ try _____18_____ find a roommate? That would make it cheaper _____19_____ both _____20_____ _____21_____.

SAM: _____22_____ _____23_____ _____24_____ is true, but right now, I don't _____25_____ _____26_____ have a roommate.

MARK: Okay. That reminds me. Hiro said that _____27_____ _____28_____ motel, there's a refrigerator _____29_____ a stove. _____30_____ _____31_____ _____32_____ _____33_____ _____34_____ find a place that has those, too, _____35_____ _____36_____?

SAM: I _____37_____ _____38_____. I _____39_____ _____40_____ find a *cheap* apartment!

MARK: Okay. Don't worry. We'll find just _____41_____ _____42_____ _____43_____ _____44_____ sooner _____45_____ later.

DISCUSSION

Work in small groups.

What's the best way to find a place to live? Explain.

Can't You Find an Apartment? **65**

21 Could You Check My Sink?

/d/ + you ⟶ *ja
/d/ + your ⟶ *jer

Part 1 INTRODUCTION

CONVERSATION

Listen to each part of the conversation: first spoken with careful (slow) pronunciation, then spoken with relaxed (fast) pronunciation.

Careful (Slow) Pronunciation

KARL: Jim, where are you? I knocked twice, but you didn't answer your door.
JIM: Karl! Could you come into the kitchen? Quick!
KARL: Oh, my gosh! Look at all of that water!
JIM: Would you get me some towels?
KARL: Sure. Did your pipe break?
JIM: I can't hear you. What did you say?
KARL: I said, "Did your pipe break?"
JIM: Yes. Could you call your brother? He's a plumber, right?
KARL: I told you he moved last year, remember?
JIM: Then could you call somebody else? This is an emergency.

Relaxed (Fast) Pronunciation

KARL: Jim, where are *ya? I knocked twice, but *cha didn't answer *yer door.
JIM: Karl! Could *ja come into the kitchen? Quick!
KARL: Oh, my gosh! Look at all *a that water!
JIM: Would *ja *git me some towels?
KARL: Sure. Did *jer pipe break?
JIM: I can't hear *ya. What did *ja say?
KARL: I said, "Did *jer pipe break?"
JIM: Yes. Could *ja call *yer brother? He's a plumber, right?
KARL: I told *ja he moved last year, remember?
JIM: Then could *ja call somebody else? This is an emergency.

TRACK 21A

Listen to the entire conversation again, spoken with relaxed (fast) pronunciation.

TRACK 21B

COMPREHENSION

Answer these questions about the conversation.

1. Where are Jim and Karl?
2. Do you think Karl is a neighbor? Explain.
3. What's Jim's problem?
4. What does he want to do?
5. Why is this an emergency?

Now, work with a partner and compare your answers.

PRACTICE

Close your book. You'll hear each part of the conversation spoken with relaxed pronunciation. Repeat each part using careful pronunciation.

TRACK 21C

Part 2 EXPANSION

COMPREHENSION

Listen to the conversation. The speakers use relaxed pronunciation. Answer the questions.

1. Is the plumber a man or a woman?
2. What's wrong with Jim's plumbing?
3. Why does Jim want the plumber to fix the plumbing cheaply?
4. Why doesn't Jim pay with a credit card?
5. What do you think will happen next?

TRACK 21D

Work with a partner. Compare your answers. Listen again if necessary.

Could You Check My Sink?

PRACTICE

Listen again. The conversation is spoken with relaxed pronunciation. Complete the sentences with the words you would hear if they were spoken with careful pronunciation. Then, listen once more and check your answers.

TRACK 21E

HELEN: I think I found ____(1)____ leak.

JIM: What did ____(2)____ say?

HELEN: I think I found ____(3)____ leak! I'm ____(4)____ ____(5)____ ____(6)____ ____(7)____ turn off ____(8)____ water! When was the last time ____(9)____ had ____(10)____ pipes checked?

JIM: I had ____(11)____ checked maybe six ____(12)____ seven years ago. Are they that bad?

HELEN: ____(13)____ kitchen pipes ____(14)____ ____(15)____ be replaced, ____(16)____ ____(17)____ really need ____(18)____ faucets changed. ____(19)____ ____(20)____ like me ____(21)____ start now?

JIM: ____(22)____ ____(23)____ ____(24)____ change the pipes? ____(25)____ ____(26)____ just fix ____(27)____?

HELEN: ____(28)____ ____(29)____ know there was a toy rabbit in ____(30)____ drain? I'm a plumber, not a magician.

JIM: Well, I don't have much money. Would ____(31)____ do it as cheaply as ____(32)____ ____(33)____?

HELEN: Of course.

(Several hours later)

HELEN: That's ____(34)____ ____(35)____ be $347.63 ____(36)____ the new pipes ____(37)____ faucets.

JIM: $347.63?

HELEN: Yes. Plus tax.

68   Chapter 21

JIM: I only have $20. _____(38)_____(39) take a credit card? Most businesses take credit cards, right?

HELEN: I'm sorry, we don't take credit cards.

JIM: Oh. Then, we've got a problem!

DISCUSSION
Work in small groups.

Is plumbing an unusual job for a woman? What's an unusual job for a man? Explain.

22 Who Have You Asked to Fly the Plane?

Deletion of Initial /h/

Wh- question words + have ⟶ *'ave

Wh- question words + has ⟶ *'as

Wh- question words + had ⟶ *'ad

What have you can also become ***Whaddaya***. A related form, ***Whadda***, can be used when *What have* is followed by either *we* or *they*. Example:

***Whadda** they done?*

Part 1 INTRODUCTION

CONVERSATION

Listen to each part of the conversation: first spoken with careful (slow) pronunciation, then spoken with relaxed (fast) pronunciation.

TRACK 22A

Careful (Slow) Pronunciation	Relaxed (Fast) Pronunciation

ELIZABETH: Well, hello! What have you been doing lately?

TOM: Oh, I've been hiking a lot. So, where has your sister been? I haven't seen her.

ELIZABETH: She's gone to Shanghai.

TOM: Shanghai? Why has she gone to Shanghai?

ELIZABETH: To visit some friends. So, who have you been hiking with?

TOM: Mostly my grandson. And how have your grandchildren been?

ELIZABETH: Great. I gave my granddaughter some skydiving lessons for her graduation.

ELIZABETH: Well, hello! *Whaddaya been *doin' lately?

TOM: Oh, I've been *hikin' a lot. So, where *'as *yer sister been? I haven't seen *'er.

ELIZABETH: She's gone *ta Shanghai.

TOM: Shanghai? Why *'as she gone *ta Shanghai?

ELIZABETH: *Ta visit some friends. So, who *'ave *ya been *hikin' with?

TOM: Mostly my grandson. *'N' how *'ave *yer grandchildren been?

ELIZABETH: Great. I gave my granddaughter some skydiving lessons *fer *'er graduation.

70 Chapter 22

TOM: Really? When had she become interested in skydiving?
ELIZABETH: Oh, a few months ago. We're, uh, doing it together.
TOM: You're jumping out of airplanes? What have your children said about that?

TOM: Really? When *'ad she become interested in skydiving?
ELIZABETH: Oh, a few months ago. We're, uh, *doin' it together.
TOM: *Yer *jumpin' out *a airplanes? *Whadda *yer children said about that?

Listen to the entire conversation again, spoken with relaxed (fast) pronunciation.

TRACK 22B

COMPREHENSION

Answer these questions about the conversation.

1. How well do you think Tom and Elizabeth know each other? Explain.
2. Where has Elizabeth's sister gone? Why?
3. How old do you think Tom and Elizabeth are? Why?
4. Do you think Elizabeth is too old to skydive? Explain.
5. Do you think Tom and Elizabeth are healthy? Explain.

Now, work with a partner and compare your answers.

PRACTICE

Close your book. You'll hear each part of the conversation spoken with relaxed pronunciation. Repeat each part using careful pronunciation.

TRACK 22C

Part 2 EXPANSION

Who Have You Asked to Fly the Plane?

COMPREHENSION

Listen to the conversation. The speakers use relaxed pronunciation. Answer the questions.

1. Where are Robert and Elizabeth?
2. What do you think the relationship between them is?
3. Who didn't like airplanes?
4. Who took the skydiving class?
5. Did Elizabeth misunderstand something? Explain.
6. How often do you think Robert and Elizabeth see each other? Explain.

Work with a partner. Compare your answers. Listen again if necessary.

TRACK 22D

PRACTICE

Listen again. The conversation is spoken with relaxed pronunciation. Complete the sentences with the words you would hear if they were spoken with careful pronunciation. Then, listen once more and check your answers.

TRACK 22E

ELIZABETH: Robert!

ROBERT: Elizabeth! _____(1)_____ _____(2)_____ _____(3)_____ _____(4)_____ at the tennis courts?

ELIZABETH: I'm with a friend. So, how _____(5)_____ _____(6)_____ been?

ROBERT: Great. How _____(7)_____ you been?

ELIZABETH: Terrific. So, _____(8)_____ _____(9)_____ _____(10)_____ been _____(11)_____ lately?

ROBERT: Oh, _____(12)_____, _____(13)_____ tennis… _____(14)_____ I've decided _____(15)_____ go skydiving again.

ELIZABETH: Really? When _____(16)_____ _____(17)_____ decided _____(18)_____ go skydiving?

ROBERT: I'm _____(19)_____ _____(20)_____ go next week. _____(21)_____ know, when my wife was alive, she wouldn't even fly in airplanes. We _____(22)_____ _____(23)_____ _____(24)_____ _____(25)_____ take trains everywhere.

ELIZABETH: When my husband was alive, he wouldn't even watch skydiving on TV. So, who _____(26)_____ _____(27)_____ decided _____(28)_____ jump with? Our skydiving teacher?

72   Chapter 22

ROBERT: No. My son.

ELIZABETH: Oh? Why ___29___ ___30___ decided ___31___ do this? I thought ___32___ didn't like skydiving.

ROBERT: Why ___33___ ___34___ thought that? He took the skydiving class after we did, ___35___ ___36___ loved it.

ELIZABETH: Why ___37___ I thought that? I ___38___ ___39___. I guess I misunderstood what ___40___ told me in class.

ROBERT: Well, maybe ___41___ didn't want me ___42___ take the class at first, but when ___43___ a son ever wanted ___44___ father ___45___ do something dangerous?

ELIZABETH: My children feel the same way. So, who ___46___ ___47___ asked ___48___ fly the plane?

ROBERT: My younger daughter.

ELIZABETH: Jane? That's great. Where ___49___ she been ___50___ flying lessons?

ROBERT: At a local airport. She just got ___51___ license. Do ___52___ ___53___ ___54___ join us?

ELIZABETH: Sure. I'd love to.

DISCUSSION

Work in small groups.

Should elderly people date? Should they hike or skydive? Explain.

23 Could I Have an Appointment with Dr. Okamoto?

Deletion of Initial /h/

Subject + **have** ⟶ *'ave
Subject + **has** ⟶ *'as
Subject + **had** ⟶ *'ad
haven't ⟶ *'aven't
hasn't ⟶ *'asn't
hadn't ⟶ *'adn't

Although Subject + *'**ave** can be pronounced *of, **have** doesn't reduce further to *a.

Part 1 INTRODUCTION

CONVERSATION

Listen to each part of the conversation: first spoken with careful (slow) pronunciation, then spoken with relaxed (fast) pronunciation.

TRACK 23A

Careful (Slow) Pronunciation

RECEPTIONIST: Hello. Dr. Okamoto's office.
TONY: This is Tony Lamotta. I have a terrible backache.
RECEPTIONIST: We have an opening tomorrow morning at 10:00.
TONY: I had to stay home from work today. You haven't got anything sooner?
RECEPTIONIST: Wait a minute. The doctor has a cancellation at 3:00 today. Can you come in then?

Relaxed (Fast) Pronunciation

RECEPTIONIST: Hello. Dr. Okamoto's office.
TONY: This is Tony Lamotta. I *ave a terrible backache.
RECEPTIONIST: We *'ave an opening tomorrow morning at 10:00.
TONY: I *'ad *ta stay home from work today. *Ya *'aven't got anything sooner?
RECEPTIONIST: Wait a minute. The doctor *'as a cancellation at 3:00 today. *Kin *ya come in then?

74 Chapter 23

TONY: She has an opening at 3:00? Thank you so much.
RECEPTIONIST: You're welcome. What kind of insurance do you have?
TONY: What kind of insurance do I have?
RECEPTIONIST: The doctors have a policy. If you don't have insurance, we can't bill you.
TONY: You mean, I'm going to have to pay her today? I hadn't planned for that.

TONY: She *'as an opening at 3:00? Thank *ya so much.
RECEPTIONIST: *Yer welcome. What kind *a insurance do *ya *'ave?
TONY: What kind *a insurance do I *'ave?
RECEPTIONIST: The doctors *'ave a policy. If *ya don't *'ave insurance, we can't bill *ya.
TONY: *Ya mean, I'm *gonna *hafta pay *'er today? I *'adn't planned *fer that.

Listen to the entire conversation again, spoken with relaxed (fast) pronunciation.

TRACK 23B

COMPREHENSION

Answer these questions about the conversation.

1. What's Tony's problem?
2. When do they first offer him an appointment?
3. Why does he want an appointment sooner?
4. Do you think Tony has medical insurance? Explain.
5. What do you think the receptionist will say next?

Now, work with a partner and compare your answers.

PRACTICE

Close your book. You'll hear each part of the conversation spoken with relaxed pronunciation. Repeat each part using careful pronunciation.

TRACK 23C

Part 2 EXPANSION

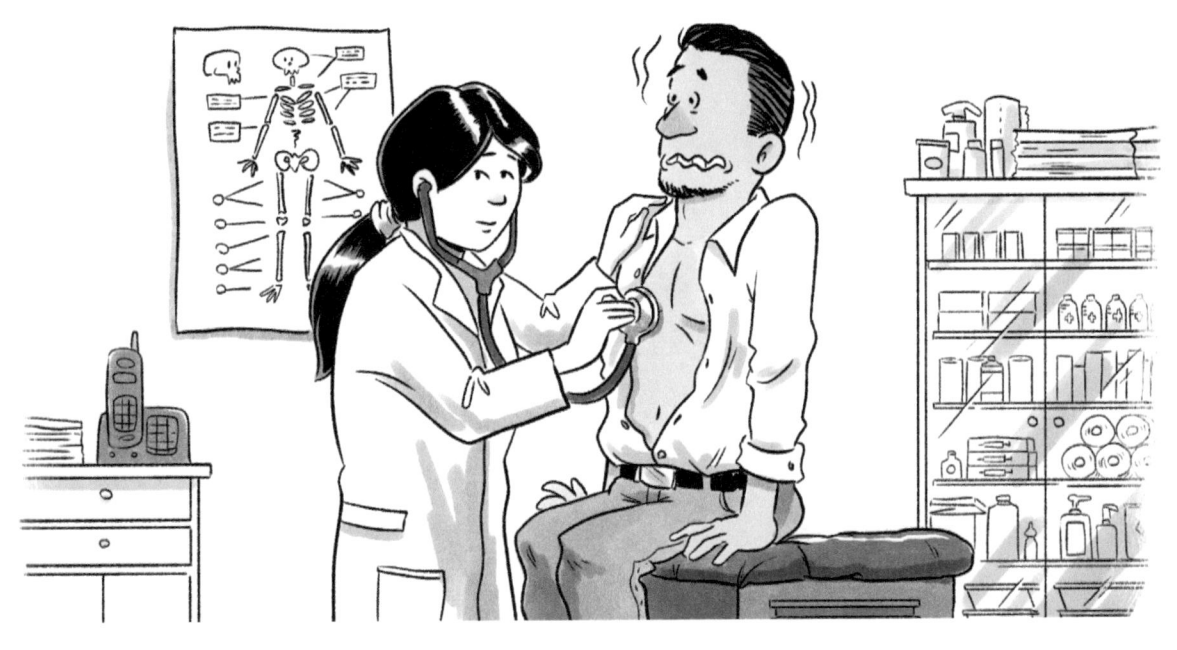

Could I Have an Appointment with Dr. Okamoto? **75**

COMPREHENSION

Listen to the conversation. The speakers use relaxed pronunciation. Answer the questions.

1. Why do you think the doctor wants to listen to Tony's heart?
2. What's too cold for Tony?
3. How old is Tony?
4. How did Tony injure his back?
5. How old was Tony when he had his son?
6. What does Tony have to do to get better?

TRACK 23D

Work with a partner. Compare your answers. Listen again if necessary.

PRACTICE

Listen again. The conversation is spoken with relaxed pronunciation. Complete the sentences with the words you would hear if they were spoken with careful pronunciation. Then, listen once more and check your answers.

TRACK 23E

DOCTOR OKAMOTO: Okay. Do ___(1)___ ___(2)___ any pain here?

TONY: No. I ___(3)___ pain there last night, but not now.

DOCTOR: Please take off ___(4)___ shirt. I ___(5)___ ___(6)___ listen ___(7)___ ___(8)___ heart.

TONY: Oh, my gosh!

DOCTOR: What's wrong? I ___(9)___ done anything yet. I'm just ___(10)___ ___(11)___ ___(12)___ heart.

TONY: Sorry. It's just cold.

DOCTOR: I'm really sorry. Sometimes, I forget ___(13)___ warm the stethoscope.

TONY: That's okay.

DOCTOR: Okay, now I want ___(14)___ ___(15)___ take a deep breath; then, breathe out. Okay, good. We ___(16)___ a couple ___(17)___ tests we need ___(18)___ do now. ___(19)___ ___(20)___ touch ___(21)___ toes ___(22)___ me?

TONY: My toes? I ___(23)___ an injured back. I ___(24)___ even touch my knees.

76 Chapter 23

DOCTOR: How old are _____(25)_____, Tony?

TONY: Forty-nine. I _____(26)_____ a birthday last month.

DOCTOR: Sometimes, as we _____(27)_____ older, we _____(28)_____ a little pain in the lower back. How is it when I touch _____(29)_____ here?

TONY: Ouch! _____(30)_____ _____(31)_____ that all older people _____(32)_____ this kind _____(33)_____ pain?

DOCTOR: No. Not as bad as this. How _____(34)_____ _____(35)_____ hurt _____(36)_____ back?

TONY: _____(37)_____ baseball with my eleven-year-old son. _____(38)_____ _____(39)_____ _____(40)_____ practice.

DOCTOR: Do _____(41)_____ usually _____(42)_____ this much pain?

TONY: Well, no. We played _____(43)_____ three hours. _____(44)_____ _____(45)_____ a play-off game soon. _____(46)_____ _____(47)_____ been in the play-offs before.

DOCTOR: Well, no baseball _____(48)_____ you _____(49)_____ awhile. _____(50)_____ _____(51)_____ _____(52)_____ _____(53)_____ _____(54)_____ rest _____(55)_____ a few weeks.

DISCUSSION

Work in small groups.

Is it better to be a younger or an older parent? Explain.

Could I Have an Appointment with Dr. Okamoto? **77**

24 I Shouldn't Have Had Three Pieces of Cake

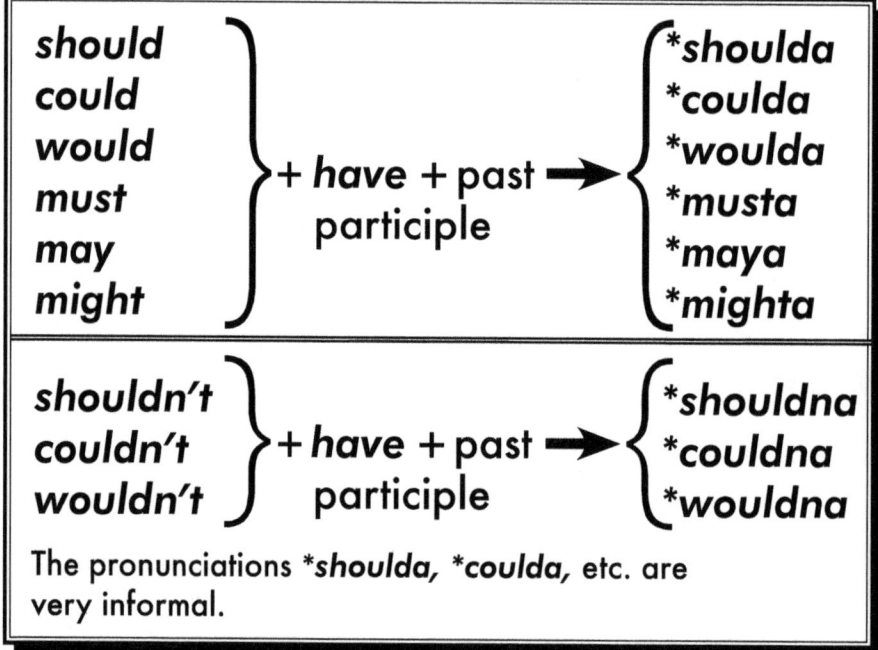

| should / could / would / must / may / might | + have + past participle → | *shoulda / *coulda / *woulda / *musta / *maya / *mighta |

| shouldn't / couldn't / wouldn't | + have + past participle → | *shouldna / *couldna / *wouldna |

The pronunciations *shoulda, *coulda, etc. are very informal.

Part 1 INTRODUCTION

CONVERSATION

Listen to each part of the conversation: first spoken with careful (slow) pronunciation, then spoken with relaxed (fast) pronunciation.

Careful (Slow) Pronunciation

HERMAN: I shouldn't have had that third piece of cake!
ZELDA: Three pieces of cake! You couldn't have eaten three pieces of cake!
HERMAN: Well, usually I wouldn't have. But since I stopped smoking, I must have started eating a little more.
ZELDA: A little? Last night, you had a whole pizza.
HERMAN: You had dinner with me. I couldn't have eaten the whole pizza.

Relaxed (Fast) Pronunciation

HERMAN: I *shouldna *'ad that third piece *a cake!
ZELDA: Three pieces *a cake! *Ya *couldna eaten three pieces *a cake!
HERMAN: Well, usually I *wouldna. But since I stopped *smokin', I *musta started *eatin' a little more.
ZELDA: A little? Last night, *ya had a whole pizza!
HERMAN: You had dinner with me. I *couldna eaten the whole pizza.

TRACK 24A

78 Chapter 24

ZELDA: Well, I may have remembered it wrong. I might have had one piece. But *you* ate most of the pizza.

HERMAN: I would have given you more if you had asked.

ZELDA: You were eating like your plane was going down, and it was your last meal. But you're right. I should have asked.

HERMAN: You could have.

ZELDA: But you wouldn't have eaten the whole thing if you hadn't been trying to stop smoking, right?

ZELDA: Well, I *maya remembered it wrong. I *mighta had one piece. But *you* ate most *a the pizza.

HERMAN: I *woulda given *ya more if *ya *'ad asked.

ZELDA: *Ya were *eatin' like *yer plane was *goin' down, *n it was *yer last meal. But *yer right. I *shoulda asked.

HERMAN: *Ya *coulda.

ZELDA: But *ya *wouldna eaten the whole thing if *ya *adn't been *tryin' *ta stop *smokin', right?

Listen to the entire conversation again, spoken with relaxed (fast) pronunciation.

TRACK 24B

COMPREHENSION

Answer these questions about the conversation.

1. What do you think the relationship between Zelda and Herman is?
2. Why is Zelda upset?
3. Why does Herman think he's eating so much?
4. Do you think it's difficult to stop smoking? Explain.

Now, work with a partner and compare your answers.

PRACTICE

Close your book. You'll hear each part of the conversation spoken with relaxed pronunciation. Repeat each part using careful pronunciation.

TRACK 24C

Part 2 EXPANSION

I Shouldn't Have Had Three Pieces of Cake

COMPREHENSION

Listen to the conversation. The speakers use relaxed pronunciation. Answer the questions.

1. What's Herman's problem?
2. What's difficult about this problem?
3. How does Zelda feel about it? Why?
4. Do you think Herman will fix his problem? Explain.

Work with a partner. Compare your answers. Listen again if necessary.

PRACTICE

Listen again. The conversation is spoken with relaxed pronunciation. Complete the sentences with the words you would hear if they were spoken with careful pronunciation. Then, listen once more and check your answers.

ZELDA: Oh no! Are ___1___ ___2___ again? ___3___ said ___4___ quit.

HERMAN: That cigarette ___5___ ___6___ been from before. A long time before.

ZELDA: It's still ___7___.

HERMAN: Oh. ___8___ right. I know I ___9___ ___10___ done it, but ___11___ ___12___ isn't easy.

ZELDA: ___13___ ___14___ ___15___ been ___16___ the patch the doctor suggested.

HERMAN: I ___17___ ___18___, but it stopped ___19___ ___20___ me.

ZELDA: Then ___21___ ___22___ ___23___ tried that special gum.

HERMAN: I ___24___ ___25___ forgotten where it was.

ZELDA: ___26___ ___27___ ___28___ forgotten. It's on the counter, next to ___29___ cigarettes.

HERMAN: Oh, yeah.

80 Chapter 24

DISCUSSION
Work in small groups.

What's the best way to quit a bad habit?

25 What Are You Doing to My Hair?

What are you ⟶ *Whacha

*Whacha is more informal than *Whaddaya.
*Whacha is occasionally used for What do you.

Part 1 INTRODUCTION

CONVERSATION

Listen to each part of the conversation: first spoken with careful (slow) pronunciation, then spoken with relaxed (fast) pronunciation.

TRACK 25A

Careful (Slow) Pronunciation	Relaxed (Fast) Pronunciation

BILL: What are you doing this afternoon?
GEORGETTE: I'm going to go to my cousin's new hair salon. He's going to do my hair.
BILL: What are you going to do to your hair? I love your hair.
GEORGETTE: I don't know. Don't you think I should change my hairstyle?
BILL: What do you want to do that for? Our hairstyles are the same.
GEORGETTE: I see what you mean. But what are you going to do about finding a job?
BILL: I don't know. What do you think I should do?
GEORGETTE: Well, maybe we should try to look a little more professional.
BILL: Why?
GEORGETTE: Well, we're both looking for jobs, and we need to change our "look."

BILL: *Whacha *doin' this afternoon?
GEORGETTE: I'm gonna go *da my cousin's new hair salon. He's gonna do my hair.
BILL: *Whacha *gonna do *da *yer hair? I love *yer hair.
GEORGETTE: I *donno. Don't *cha think I should change my hairstyle?
BILL: *Whacha *wanna do that for? Our hairstyles are the same.
GEORGETTE: I see what *cha mean. But *whacha *gonna do about *findin' a job?
BILL: I *donno. *Whaddaya think I should do?
GEORGETTE: Well, maybe we should try *da look a little more professional.
BILL: Why?
GEORGETTE: Well, we're both *lookin' *fer jobs, 'n' we need *ta change our "look."

Listen to the entire conversation again, spoken with relaxed (fast) pronunciation.

TRACK 25B

Chapter 25

COMPREHENSION

Answer these questions about the conversation.

1. What do you think the relationship between Bill and Georgette is? Explain.
2. Do Bill and Georgette like their hairstyles? Explain.
3. What does Georgette think Bill should do to get a job?
4. Do you think this is a good idea? Explain.
5. How old do you think Bill and Georgette are? Why?

Now, work with a partner and compare your answers.

PRACTICE

Close your book. You'll hear each part of the conversation spoken with relaxed pronunciation. Repeat each part using careful pronunciation.

TRACK 25C

Part 2 EXPANSION

COMPREHENSION

Listen to the conversation. The speakers use relaxed pronunciation. Answer the questions.

1. Did Georgette's cousin cut off a lot of hair? Explain.
2. Why do you think George says, "Hair grows so fast"?
3. Do you think Georgette should have let George continue to cut her hair? Explain.
4. What do you think George's biggest problem is?
5. Would you go to George to get your hair cut? Explain.

TRACK 25D

Work with a partner. Compare your answers. Listen again if necessary.

What Are You Doing to My Hair?

PRACTICE

Listen again. The conversation is spoken with relaxed pronunciation. Complete the sentences with the words you would hear if they were spoken with careful pronunciation. Then, listen once more and check your answers.

TRACK 25E

GEORGETTE: George, __(1)__ __(2)__ __(3)__ __(4)__ back there?

GEORGE: I'm __(5)__ __(6)__ __(7)__ told me __(8)__ do. I'm __(9)__ __(10)__ hair.

GEORGETTE: I didn't say __(11)__ cut it! I said __(12)__ trim it. Look, __(13)__ my cousin, __(14)__ I love __(15)__, but are __(16)__ sure __(17)__ know __(18)__ __(19)__ __(20)__?

GEORGE: Don't worry. Short hair is very popular this year.

GEORGETTE: How much did __(21)__ cut off?

GEORGE: Not much. Just six __(22)__ seven inches.

GEORGETTE: Oh. __(23)__ __(24)__ __(25)__ __(26)__ off the top now?

GEORGE: About four __(27)__ five inches.

GEORGETTE: I told __(28)__ two inches!

GEORGE: Oh, hair grows so fast. __(29)__ __(30)__ __(31)__ look great.

GEORGETTE: I __(32)__ __(33)__ __(34)__ __(35)__ __(36)__ __(37)__ __(38)__ do __(39)__ the bangs?

GEORGE: I've __(40)__ __(41)__ even __(42)__ out a little.

GEORGETTE: __(43)__ __(44)__ __(45)__ __(46)__ now?

84 Chapter 25

GEORGE: I'm just ___47___ this big... piece... here. ___48___ don't need ___49___ worry. Hair grows so fast.

GEORGETTE: Well, ___50___ ___51___ ___52___ decided ___53___ do ___54___ the sides ___55___ my hair? Maybe it'll look better when it's finished.

GEORGE: It *is* finished.

DISCUSSION
Work in small groups.

How should people look when they go on a job interview or start a new job? Which things are the most important? Why?

26 Give Me a Paintbrush

let me ➡ *lemme

give me ➡ *gimme

*Lemme and *gimme are very informal.

Part 1 INTRODUCTION

CONVERSATION

Listen to each part of the conversation: first spoken with careful (slow) pronunciation, then spoken with relaxed (fast) pronunciation.

TRACK 26A

Careful (Slow) Pronunciation	Relaxed (Fast) Pronunciation

DAN: My brother's going to give me some paint for my birthday.

LISA: Let me guess. You're finally going to paint your living room.

DAN: Yeah. Can you give me some advice? I can't decide on a color.

LISA: Well, I used to work in a paint store. Let me see the color samples.

DAN: Okay. I have to choose from these.

LISA: No problem. Give me the samples and tell me what colors you like.

DAN: Well, let me see the grays. What do you think about dark gray?

LISA: It's too dark for me. Let me show you this light brown. Do you like it?

DAN: My brother's *gonna *gimme some paint *fer my birthday.

LISA: *Lemme guess. *Yer finally gonna paint *cher living room.

DAN: Yeah. *Kin *ya *gimme some advice? I can't decide on a color.

LISA: Well, I *useta work in a paint store. *Lemme see the color samples.

DAN: Okay. I *hafta choose from these.

LISA: No problem. *Gimme the samples *'n' tell me what colors *ya like.

DAN: Well, *lemme see the grays. *Whaddaya think about dark gray?

LISA: It's too dark *fer me. *Lemme show *ya this light brown. Do *ya like it?

86 Chapter 26

DAN: I don't know. Give me a minute to think about it.
LISA: Did you see this beautiful yellow? We should have looked at this one first.

DAN: I donno. *Gimme a minute *ta think about it.
LISA: Did *ja see this beautiful yellow? We *shoulda looked at this one first.

Listen to the entire conversation again, spoken with relaxed (fast) pronunciation.

TRACK 26B

COMPREHENSION

Answer these questions about the conversation.

1. What do you think the relationship between Dan and Lisa is? Explain.
2. Why do you think Dan is getting paint for his birthday?
3. Who do you think knows more about choosing colors to paint a room, Dan or Lisa? Explain.
4. What do you think is the best color to paint Dan's living room? Why?

Now, work with a partner and compare your answers.

PRACTICE

Close your book. You'll hear each part of the conversation spoken with relaxed pronunciation. Repeat each part using careful pronunciation.

TRACK 26C

Part 2 EXPANSION

Give Me a Paintbrush **87**

COMPREHENSION

Listen to the conversation. The speakers use relaxed pronunciation. Answer the questions.

1. What's the relationship between Dan and Leonard?
2. What are the steps in painting a room?
3. Does Leonard know how to paint a room? Explain.
4. Why do you think Dan felt that Leonard was a *house* painter?
5. Do you think Leonard made a lot of money as an artist? Why or why not?

Work with a partner. Compare your answers. Listen again if necessary.

TRACK 26D

PRACTICE

Listen again. The conversation is spoken with relaxed pronunciation. Complete the sentences with the words you would hear if they were spoken with careful pronunciation. Then, listen once more and check your answers.

TRACK 26E

DAN: I ___(1)___ ___(2)___ paint our living room, Leonard. Do ___(3)___ know how ___(4)___ paint?

LEONARD: Do I know how ___(5)___ paint? Do *I* know how ___(6)___ paint? Now, I sell computers ___(7)___ pay my half ___(8)___ our rent, but I ___(9)___ ___(10)___ be a painter.

DAN: ___(11)___ did? Great! I ___(12)___ ___(13)___ anything about painting.

LEONARD: Here, Dan. ___(14)___ ___(15)___ open that paint can.

DAN: Oh, my gosh! ___(16)___ spilled it!

LEONARD: ___(17)___ ___(18)___ a rag. I'll clean it up. See? No problem. ___(19)___ ___(20)___ a paintbrush. Let's ___(21)___ started.

DAN: Shouldn't we cover the furniture with sheets first? We don't ___(22)___ ___(23)___ ___(24)___ paint on our furniture.

LEONARD: Yes. Good idea. ___(25)___ ___(26)___ help ___(27)___ ___(28)___ ___(29)___ the other corner ___(30)___ the sheet.

LEONARD: _____ _____ a paintbrush. Let's
         31   32
_____ started.
 33
DAN: But, shouldn't we sand the walls first?

LEONARD: Sand the walls? Good idea.

(Thirty minutes later)

LEONARD: Okay. We sanded the walls. What a great idea! Now, _____
                                                              34
_____ a paintbrush. _____ _____ paint this
 35   36   37
wall. *You* paint the other one.

DAN: Sure. _____ the painter.
            38

(An hour later)

DAN: My wall's finished. _____ _____ see
                          39   40
_____.
 41

LEONARD: There it is. Isn't it beautiful?

DAN: _____ said _____ were a painter! _____
      42   43   44
_____ _____ painted on _____ wall?
 45   46   47

LEONARD: Cheese. The yellow paint made me think _____ cheese.
                                                   48
_____ _____ explain. I was never a *house* painter. I
 49   50
_____ _____ be an *artist*.
 51   52

DISCUSSION
Work in small groups.

What are the best colors for a room where you spend a lot of time? Explain.

27 I Couldn't Take the Test Because I Was Sick

Deletion of Syllables:

about → *'bout

because → *'cause

come on → *c'mon

*'Bout, *'cause, and *c'mon are very informal.

Part 1 INTRODUCTION

CONVERSATION

Listen to each part of the conversation: first spoken with careful (slow) pronunciation, then spoken with relaxed (fast) pronunciation.

TRACK 27A

Careful (Slow) Pronunciation	Relaxed (Fast) Pronunciation

JUAN: Can you give me a ride to school?

MRS. RODRIGUEZ: I can't because I have to finish a report before I leave.

JUAN: Well, how long is it going to take you?

MRS. RODRIGUEZ: Oh, about thirty or forty minutes.

JUAN: Come on, Mom. I don't want to be late for my makeup test.

MRS. RODRIGUEZ: Makeup test? What are you talking about?

JUAN: I forgot to tell you. I missed a test because I was sick.

MRS. RODRIGUEZ: You missed the test when you had the flu?

JUAN: Yeah. Mom, can you give me some money, too? I won't have time to make my lunch now—

JUAN: "Kin *ya *gimme a ride "ta school?

MRS. RODRIGUEZ: I can't *'cause I *hafta finish a report before I leave.

JUAN: Well, how long is it *gonna take *ya?

MRS. RODRIGUEZ: Oh, *'bout thirty *er forty minutes.

JUAN: *C'mon, Mom. I don't *wanna be late *fer my makeup test.

MRS. RODRIGUEZ: Makeup test? *Whaddaya *talkin' *'bout?

JUAN: I forgot *ta tell *ya. I missed a test *'cause I was sick.

MRS. RODRIGUEZ: *Ya missed the test when "ya *'ad the flu?

JUAN: Yeah. Mom, *kin *ya *gimme some money, too? I won't have time *ta make my lunch now—

MRS. RODRIGUEZ: -because of the makeup test. Here's your money. Come on. Let's go.

MRS. RODRIGUEZ: *'cause *a the makeup test. Here's "yer money. *C'mon. Let's go.

Listen to the entire conversation again, spoken with relaxed (fast) pronunciation.

TRACK 27B

COMPREHENSION

Answer these questions about the conversation.

1. Why is Juan taking a makeup test?
2. Why does he want a ride to school?
3. Why does he need money?
4. What's Juan's last name?
5. What time of day do you think it is? Explain.
6. Do you think his mother should drive him to school? Explain.

Now, work with a partner and compare your answers.

PRACTICE

Close your book. You'll hear each part of the conversation spoken with relaxed pronunciation. Repeat each part using careful pronunciation.

TRACK 27C

Part 2 EXPANSION

I Couldn't Take the Test Because I Was Sick   **91**

COMPREHENSION

Listen to the conversation. The speakers use relaxed pronunciation. Answer the questions.

1. Where are Juan and Martin? Explain.
2. What are they going to do? Why?
3. What does Martin have to do to get a scholarship? Why?
4. Does Juan work? Why or why not?

Work with a partner. Compare your answers. Listen again if necessary.

TRACK 27D

PRACTICE

Listen again. The conversation is spoken with relaxed pronunciation. Complete the sentences with the words you would hear if they were spoken with careful pronunciation. Then, listen once more and check your answers.

TRACK 27E

MARTIN: Hi, Juan. Where are _____(1) _____(2)?

JUAN: Well, I _____(3) _____(4) take a makeup test in our history class _____(5) I was sick.

MARTIN: A lot _____(6) people missed the test. _____(7) _____(8). I _____(9) _____(10) take it, too.

JUAN: You missed it, too?

MARTIN: Yeah.

JUAN: How long do _____(11) think it'll take?

MARTIN: _____(12) an hour.

JUAN: So, did _____(13) study?

MARTIN: I studied a lot. I _____(14) _____(15) _____(16) an "A" in this class _____(17) I _____(18) _____(19) _____(20) a scholarship. I _____(21) _____(22) go _____(23) graduate school.

JUAN: I _____(24) a scholarship, Martin, but I still _____(25) _____(26) work _____(27) college is so expensive.

MARTIN: _____(28) right. I've been _____(29) _____(30) _____(31) a year. If I _____(32) a scholarship, I'll still

92   Chapter 27

_____ _____ work, but my parents won't
   33   34
_____ _____ pay so much. Anyway, _____
   35   36   37
_____. Let's go. We're _____ _____ be late.
   38   39   40

JUAN: *You* go ahead. I've _____ _____ go
                                41   42
_____ my locker _____ I've _____
   43   44   45
_____ _____ some books.
   46   47

MARTIN: How long will _____ be?
                           48

JUAN: _____ ten minutes.
         49

MARTIN: Okay. _____ See at the test.
                   50

JUAN: Yeah. See _____ there.
                     51

DISCUSSION

Work in small groups.

Who do you think should pay for a student's education? Explain.

28 Been to the Circus Lately?

Deletion of Words in Questions:

Do you **want some**... → **Want some**...
Are you **going to** see... → ***Gonna see**...
Would you **like to**... → **Like to**...
Have you **seen the**... → **Seen the**...

These forms are very informal. We can delete the first one or two words of these questions. Examples:

Do you want some popcorn?
*Ya want some popcorn? OR **Want some** popcorn?

Have you seen any good movies?
*Ya seen any good movies? OR **Seen any** good movies?

Part 1 INTRODUCTION

CONVERSATION

Listen to each part of the conversation: first spoken with careful (slow) pronunciation, then spoken with relaxed (fast) pronunciation.

TRACK 28A

Careful (Slow) Pronunciation	Relaxed (Fast) Pronunciation
PAUL: Have you seen any good shows for kids lately?	PAUL: Seen any good shows *fer kids lately?
ANNE: Are you thinking about your son, Joey?	ANNE: *Ya *thinkin' *'bout *cher son, Joey?
PAUL: Yeah. Do you know what I did last week?	PAUL: Yeah. Know what I did last week?
ANNE: What did you do?	ANNE: What did *ja do?
PAUL: I got tickets to see the circus. Have you been to the circus lately?	PAUL: I got tickets *ta see the circus. Been *ta the circus lately?
ANNE: No. I've never been to the circus.	ANNE: No. I've never been *ta the circus.
PAUL: Would you like to go with us? I really want Joey to meet you.	PAUL: Like *ta go with us? I really want Joey *da meet *cha.

94 Chapter 28

ANNE: Sounds great. Are you going to leave early?
PAUL: I was thinking about leaving around 9:00 A.M. Do you want to leave earlier?
ANNE: No, that's fine. Do you need me to bring anything?

ANNE: Sounds great. *Ya *gonna leave early?
PAUL: I was *thinkin' *'bout *leavin' around 9:00 A.M. *Ya *wanna leave earlier?
ANNE: No, that's fine. Need me *da bring anything?

Listen to the entire conversation again, spoken with relaxed (fast) pronunciation.

COMPREHENSION

Answer these questions about the conversation.

1. What do you think the relationship between Paul and Anne is? Explain.
2. Do you think they've known each other a long time? Explain.
3. Where are they planning to go? Why?
4. When do you think the performance is: in the morning, afternoon, or evening? Explain.

Now, work with a partner and compare your answers.

PRACTICE

Close your book. You'll hear each part of the conversation spoken with relaxed pronunciation. Repeat each part using careful pronunciation.

Part 2 EXPANSION

COMPREHENSION

Listen to the conversation. The speakers use relaxed pronunciation. Answer the questions.

1. How old do you think Joey is? Why?
2. Do you think Joey likes Anne at first? Explain.
3. Do you think Joey's mother really said he shouldn't see the tigers? Explain.
4. Do you think Joey's behaving badly? Explain.
5. Do you think Joey's feelings about Anne change? Explain.

Work with a partner. Compare your answers. Listen again if necessary.

PRACTICE

Listen again. The conversation is spoken with relaxed pronunciation. Complete the sentences with the words you would hear if they were spoken with careful pronunciation. Then, listen once more and check your answers.

TRACK 28D

TRACK 28E

PAUL: Anne, this is Joey. Joey, I ___(1)___ ___(2)___ ___(3)___ meet Anne. We're ___(4)___ ___(5)___ have a great time today.

ANNE: Nice ___(6)___ ___(7)___ ___(8)___.

JOEY: Hi.

ANNE: This is my first time at the circus ___(9)___ I'm really excited. (___(10)___ ___(11)___) ___(12)___ ___(13)___ see the elephants, Joey?

JOEY: No.

ANNE: Okay. ___(14)___ like animals, ___(15)___ ___(16)___?

JOEY: I ___(17)___ ___(18)___.

PAUL: Joey.

ANNE: It's okay, Paul. (*to Joey*) (___(19)___ ___(20)___) ___(21)___ ___(22)___ have a hot dog?

JOEY: No, thanks.

ANNE: Well, (___(23)___ ___(24)___) ___(25)___ the tigers before? They're really exciting ___(26)___ watch. ___(27)___ ___(28)___. I'll take ___(29)___ ___(30)___ see ___(31)___.

JOEY: My mom doesn't want me _____(32)_____ see the tigers.

ANNE: But this is the circus.

PAUL: (*to Anne*) He's just a little shy. Give _____(33)_____ some time. (*to Joey*) (_____(34)_____ _____(35)_____) _____(36)_____ what I _____(37)_____ _____(38)_____ do?

JOEY: What?

PAUL: I _____(39)_____ _____(40)_____ see the clowns.

JOEY: Yeah! Let's see the clowns! (*to Anne*) (_____(41)_____) _____(42)_____ _____(43)_____ _____(44)_____ come with us?

ANNE: (_____(45)_____ _____(46)_____) _____(47)_____ me _____(48)_____ come with _____(49)_____?

JOEY: Yeah.

DISCUSSION
Work in small groups.

Do you think a husband and wife should stay married forever if they have children?

29 Where Are Your Extra-Large Hats?

Unusual Contractions:

What are	→	*What're
What will	→	*What'll
Where are	→	*Where're
Where will	→	*Where'll
Why are	→	*Why're
Why will	→	*Why'll

Part 1 INTRODUCTION

CONVERSATION

Listen to each part of the conversation: first spoken with careful (slow) pronunciation, then spoken with relaxed (fast) pronunciation.

TRACK 29A

Careful (Slow) Pronunciation

HENRY: What are you doing?
FRANK: I'm looking for stores that sell extra- large hats.
HENRY: Why are you looking for a hat?
FRANK: I'm going to go to a soccer game. If I can't find a hat, what will I wear to protect my head?
HENRY: Why will you need an *extra-large* hat?
FRANK: Because I have a really big head.
HENRY: No, you don't. Anyway, where will you be sitting?
FRANK: In the stands. In the sun. Where are some good hat stores?

Relaxed (Fast) Pronunciation

HENRY: *What're *ya *doin'?
FRANK: I'm lookin' *fer stores that sell extra-large hats.
HENRY: *Why're *ya *lookin' *fer a hat?
FRANK: I'm *gonna go *da a soccer game. If I *can't find a hat, *what'll I wear *ta protect my head?
HENRY: *Why'll *ya need an *extra-large* hat?
FRANK: *'Cause I *'ave a really big head.
HENRY: No, *ya don't. Anyway, *where'll *ya be *sittin'?
FRANK: In the stands. In the sun. *Where're some good hat stores?

HENRY: I don't know, but why are you doing this now? You should have done it a few days ago.

FRANK: What are you talking about? I started looking for a hat last week.

HENRY: I *donno, but *why're *ya *doin' this now? *Ya *shoulda done it a few days ago.

FRANK: *What're *ya *talkin' *'bout? I started "lookin' *fer a hat last week.

Listen to the entire conversation again, spoken with relaxed (fast) pronunciation.

TRACK 29B

COMPREHENSION

Answer these questions about the conversation.

1. What do you think the relationship between Frank and Henry is? Explain.
2. What's Frank looking for?
3. Why does he need an extra-large hat?
4. When did Frank start looking for a hat?

Now, work with a partner and compare your answers.

PRACTICE

Close your book. You'll hear each part of the conversation spoken with relaxed pronunciation. Repeat each part using careful pronunciation.

TRACK 29C

Part 2 EXPANSION

Where Are Your Extra-Large Hats? **99**

COMPREHENSION

Listen to the conversation. The speakers use relaxed pronunciation. Answer the questions.

1. What's Frank trying to do?
2. Why doesn't Frank call one of the departments directly?
3. How many departments does Frank talk to?
4. Why does each department transfer him to another department?
5. How do you think Frank feels at the end of the telephone call? Why?

Work with a partner. Compare your answers. Listen again if necessary.

TRACK 29D

PRACTICE

Listen again. The conversation is spoken with relaxed pronunciation. Complete the sentences with the words you would hear if they were spoken with careful pronunciation. Then, listen once more and check your answers.

TRACK 29E

RECORDING: La Porte Department Store. ___(1)___ our main directory, please press 1 now. Thank you. ___(2)___ speak ___(3)___ an operator, please stay on the line. Thank you.

OPERATOR: May I help ___(4)___?

FRANK: Yes. ___(5)___ ___(6)___ I find extra-large hats?

OPERATOR: I'll ___(7)___ ___(8)___ ___(9)___ Men's Clothing.

FRANK: Thank you.

MEN'S CLOTHING: Men's Clothing. ___(10)___ I help ___(11)___?

FRANK: Yes. ___(12)___ ___(13)___ ___(14)___ extra-large hats?

MEN'S CLOTHING: Extra-large hats? Hmm. I'm ___(15)___ ___(16)___ ___(17)___ ___(18)___ transfer ___(19)___ ___(20)___ Accessories.

ACCESSORIES: Accessories. ___(21)___ I help ___(22)___?

FRANK: Uh, ___(23)___ ___(24)___ I find extra-large hats?

ACCESSORIES: Extra-large hats? ___(25)___ ___(26)___ transfer ___(27)___ ___(28)___ Sporting Goods.

SPORTING GOODS: Sporting Goods. May I help ___(29)___?

Chapter 29

Frank: _____(30)_____ _____(31)_____ _____(32)_____ operators transferring me all over the store?

Sporting Goods: I'm sorry, sir. _____(33)_____ _____(34)_____ _____(35)_____ _____(36)_____ for?

Frank: Extra-large hats. _____(37)_____ _____(38)_____ I find _____(39)_____?

Sporting Goods: I'm sorry. I'll _____(40)_____ _____(41)_____ transfer _____(42)_____ _____(43)_____ Men's Clothing.

Frank: What? _____(44)_____ _____(45)_____ I _____(46)_____ _____(47)_____ be transferred _____(48)_____ Men's Clothing? I just talked _____(49)_____ _____(50)_____. I've been _____(51)_____ _____(52)_____ people all over _____(53)_____ store. _____(54)_____ _____(55)_____ I _____(56)_____ _____(57)_____ do _____(58)_____ find an extra-large hat?

Sporting Goods: We don't sell extra-large hats in my department. I'm really sorry. I'll transfer _____(59)_____ _____(60)_____ the operator. Maybe she _____(61)_____ help _____(62)_____

Recording: Our lines are all busy. _____(63)_____ call is important _____(64)_____ us. Please stay on the line.

Frank: I got disconnected! I _____(65)_____ believe it!

DISCUSSION

Work in small groups.

Is the telephone the best way to get information? Why or why not? What are other ways to get information about department stores? Explain.

Where Are Your Extra-Large Hats? **101**

30 When Will Your TV Program Be Over?

Unusual Contractions:

Who are	→	*Who're
Who will	→	*Who'll
When are	→	*When're
When will	→	*When'll
How are	→	*How're
How will	→	*How'll

Part 1 INTRODUCTION

CONVERSATION

Listen to each part of the conversation: first spoken with careful (slow) pronunciation, then spoken with relaxed (fast) pronunciation.

TRACK 30A

Careful (Slow) Pronunciation

ELLEN: How will we get this box inside of the house? We'll have to ask the kids to help us.

DAVID: How are they going to help us? They're not even home.

ELLEN: Oh, I forgot. So, when will we tell them your parents gave them their spare TV?

DAVID: Come on. Let's get it inside. We'll talk about that later.

ELLEN: Who will set up the TV? I don't know how to do that.

DAVID: You don't? What do we need to do?

ELLEN: It's in a box. We've got to ask somebody.

DAVID: Who are we going to ask?

Relaxed (Fast) Pronunciation

ELLEN: *How'll we *git this box inside *a the house? We'll *hafta ask the kids *ta help us.

DAVID: *How're they *gonna help us? They're not even home.

ELLEN: Oh, I forgot. So, *when'll we tell *'em *yer parents gave *'em their spare TV?

DAVID: *C'mon. Let's *git it inside. We'll talk 'bout that later.

ELLEN: *Who'll set up the TV? I *donno how *da do that.

DAVID: *Ya don't? *Whadda we need *ta do?

ELLEN: It's in a box. We've *gotta ask somebody.

DAVID: *Who're we *gonna ask?

ELLEN: The kids. After all, Joan's going to be fifteen and Keith is almost sixteen.

DAVID: The kids? When are kids shown how to set up the cable and all of that?

ELLEN: The kids. After all, Joan's *gonna be fifteen 'n' Keith is almost sixteen.

DAVID: The kids? *When're kids shown how *da set up the cable *'n' all *a that?

Listen to the entire conversation again, spoken with relaxed (fast) pronunciation.

TRACK 30B

COMPREHENSION

Answer these questions about the conversation.

1. What do you think the relationship between Ellen and David is?
2. Is the TV new or old? Explain.
3. What do you know about Joan and Keith?
4. Do Ellen and David both have confidence in their children? Explain.

Now, work with a partner and compare your answers.

PRACTICE

Close your book. You'll hear each part of the conversation spoken with relaxed pronunciation. Repeat each part using careful pronunciation.

TRACK 30C

Part 2 EXPANSION

When Will Your TV Program Be Over?

COMPREHENSION

Listen to the conversation. The speakers use relaxed pronunciation. Answer the questions.

1. Who set up the TV?
2. Why do you think Keith wants to watch *Accountants from Mars*?
3. Why do you think Joan wants to watch *Teen Issues*?
4. Why do Joan and Keith have to agree on a program?
5. What did they finally agree to watch? Why?
6. Do you think Joan and Keith get along well? Explain.

TRACK 30D

Work with a partner. Compare your answers. Listen again if necessary.

PRACTICE

Listen again. The conversation is spoken with relaxed pronunciation. Complete the sentences with the words you would hear if they were spoken with careful pronunciation. Then, listen once more and check your answers.

TRACK 30E

JOAN: I'm the one who set up the TV, Keith. _____(1)_____ _____(2)_____ _____(3)_____ _____(4)_____ _____(5)_____ be done with _____(6)_____ program?

KEITH: Shh! I'm _____(7)_____ *Accountants from Mars*.

JOAN: So. _____(8)_____ _____(9)_____ it be over? I _____(10)_____ _____(11)_____ watch something.

KEITH: _____(12)_____ _____(13)_____ _____(14)_____ _____(15)_____ _____(16)_____ watch?

JOAN: *Teen Issues*.

KEITH: Oh, no! I'm not _____(17)_____ _____(18)_____ watch a bunch _____(19)_____ girls _____(20)_____ _____(21)_____ how they feel.

JOAN: _____(22)_____ know, we're _____(23)_____ _____(24)_____ share this TV.

KEITH: _____(26)_____ we _____(27)_____ _____(28)_____ do that?

JOAN: _____(29)_____ could watch *Teen Issues*.

KEITH: No. I'd rather _____(30)_____ surgery. *You* could watch *Accountants from Mars*.

104 Chapter 30

JOAN: No. I really couldn't.

KEITH: Well, I offered ___(31)___ a compromise.

JOAN: ___(32)___ ___(33)___ ___(34)___ ___(35)___? That was no compromise.

KEITH: Look, we ___(36)___ ___(37)___ agree on a program.

JOAN: ___(38)___ ___(39)___ we do that?

KEITH: Well, I guess we've ___(40)___ ___(41)___ find something we both like.

JOAN: Yeah, right. ___(42)___ ___(43)___ decide if we ___(44)___ agree?

KEITH: We've ___(45)___ ___(46)___ agree.

JOAN: Okay. (___(47)___ ___(48)___) ___(49)___ Music Fever?

KEITH: Is that the one where they let all ___(50)___ these people with terrible voices sing?

JOAN: Yeah.

KEITH: I love that show!

DISCUSSION

Work in small groups.

What's your favorite television program? Why?

When Will Your TV Program Be Over? **105**

Test Yourself

Each of the following ten tests gives additional practice with reduced forms that are often confused. Take each test after you complete the chapter that is mentioned. When you finish *Whaddaya Say?* take all ten tests together to reinforce your understanding of spoken English.

Test 1: Do *ya/Are *ya   (Do after Chapter 5.)

Listen to the short conversation. Which do you hear: *Do you* or *Are you*? Circle the correct words.

1. Do you   Are you
2. Do you   Are you
3. Do you   Are you
4. Do you   Are you
5. Do you   Are you

TEST 1

Test 2: *wanna/*gonna   (Do after Chapter 9.)

Listen to the short conversation. Which do you hear: *want to* or *going to*? Circle the correct words.

1. want to   going to
2. want to   going to
3. want to   going to
4. want to   going to
5. want to   going to
   want to   going to

TEST 2

Test 3: *kin/can't   (Do after Chapter 10.)

Listen to the short conversation. Which do you hear: can or can't? Circle the correct word.

1. can   can't
2. can   can't
   can   can't
3. can   can't
   can   can't
4. can   can't
5. can   can't
   can   can't

TEST 3

106 Test Yourself

Test 4: *hafta/*hasta (Do after Chapter 14.)

Listen to the short conversation. Which do you hear: *have* to or *has* to? Circle the correct words.

1. have to   has to
2. have to   has to
     has to   has to
3. have to   has to
4. have to   has to

TEST 4

Test 5: *'im/*'em (Do after Chapter 16.)

Listen to the short conversation. Which do you hear: *him* or *them*? Circle the correct word.

1. him   them
2. him   them
3. him   them
4. him   them
     him   them
5. him   them
     him   them

TEST 5

Test 6: *'n'/*er (Do after Chapter 18.)

Listen to the short conversation. Which do you hear *and* or *or*? Circle the correct word.

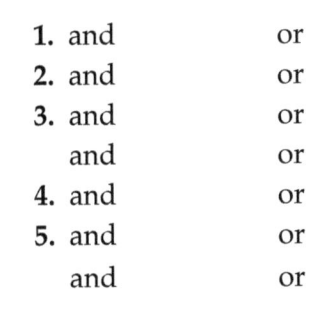

1. and   or
2. and   or
3. and   or
     and   or
4. and   or
5. and   or
     and   or

TEST 6

Test 7: *er/*fer/*er (Do after Chapter 18.)

Listen to the short conversation. Which do you hear: *or*, *for*, or *her*? Circle the correct word.

1. or   for   her
    or   for   her
2. or   for   her
3. or   for   her
    or   for   her
4. or   for   her
    or   for   her
5. or   for   her

TEST 7

Test Yourself **107**

Test 8: *Whaddaya (Do after Chapter 22.)

Listen to the short conversation. Which do you hear: *What do you, What are you,* **or** *What have you?* **Circle the correct words.**

1. What do you   What are you   What have you
2. What do you   What are you   What have you
3. What do you   what are you   what have you
4. What do you   What are you   What have you
5. What do you   What are you   What have you

Test 9: *'ave/*'as/*'ad (Do after Chapter 23.)

Listen to the short conversation. Which do you hear: *have, has,* **or** *had?* **Circle the correct word.**

1. have   has   had
2. have   has   had
   have   has   had
3. have   has   had
   have   has   had
4. have   has   had
   have   has   had

Test 10: *shoulda/* shouldna
*coulda/*couldna
*woulda/*wouldna   (Do after Chapter 24.)

Listen to the short conversation. Which do you hear: *should have, shouldn't have; could have, couldn't have; would have* **or** *wouldn't have?* **Circle the correct words.**

1. should have   shouldn't have
   shouldn't have   shouldn't have
2. couldn't have   couldn't have
3. would have   wouldn't have
   should have   shouldn't have
4. could have   couldn't have
   would have   wouldn't have
5. could have   couldn't have

Test Yourself Audio Script

Test 1: Do *ya/Are *ya

Listen to the short conversation. Which do you hear: *Do you* or *Are you*? Circle the correct words.

1. MALE: Do you like the eggs?
   FEMALE: Oh, yeah!
2. MALE: Are you finished?
   FEMALE: Yeah.
3. MALE: Do you want anything else?
   FEMALE: No.
4. MALE: Do you want the check?
   FEMALE: The check?
5. MALE: Yeah. Are you paying by credit card?
   FEMALE Uh, no. Cash.

Test 2: *wanna/*gonna

Listen to the short conversation. Which do you hear: *want to* or *going to*? Circle the correct words.

1. TEENAGER: I want to use your credit card.
2. MOM: You're not going to use my credit card.
3. TEENAGER: I'm not going to spend much.
4. MOM: You're not going to spend *anything*.
5. TEENAGER: I just want to buy a jacket. I don't want to spend a lot. Really.

Test 3: *kin/*can't

Listen to the short conversation. Which do you hear: *can* or *can't*? Circle the correct word.

1. MALE#1: Can you sing opera?
2. MALE #1: You can't sing opera, can you?
3. MALE #2: No, I can't, but I can dance.
4. MALE #1: Can you tap dance?
5. MALE #2: Well, no, I can't, but I can learn.

Test 4: *hafta/*hasta

Listen to the short conversation. Which do you hear: *have to* or *has to*? Circle the correct words.

1. FEMALE #1: What do you have to do?
2. FEMALE #2: I have to help my brother. He has to write a report.
3. FEMALE #1: He has to write a report?
4. FEMALE #2: Yes, and I have to help him.

Test 5: *im/*'em

Listen to the short conversation. Which do you hear: *him* or *them*? Circle the correct word.

1. FEMALE: Tell him what you want.
2. MALE: I can't tell him. I need to tell the whole class.
3. FEMALE: Okay, tell them what you want.
4. MALE: I don't want to tell them now. I'll tell them later.
5. FEMALE: Oh, all right. Tell him when you tell all of them.

Test 6: *'n'/*er

Listen to the short conversation. Which do you hear: *and* **or** *or*?
Circle the correct word.

1. MALE: I want some chips and dip for the party.
2. FEMALE: Do you want cheese or onion dip?
3. MALE: Onion dip. And how about some sandwiches and sodas?
4. FEMALE: Do you want turkey sandwiches or chicken?
5. MALE: Chicken. And I want them on wheat or rye bread

Test 7: *er/*fer/*'er

Listen to the short conversation. Which do you hear: *or*, *for*, **or** *her*?
Circle the correct words.

1. FEMALE: Do you want to go with her, or should I?
2. MALE: Does she want to go shopping, or does she want to go to a movie?
3. FEMALE: She wants to go shopping for an hour or two.
4. MALE: I'll go shopping with her. I'd like to do something for a few hours.
5. FEMALE: All right. I'll tell her.

Test 8: *Whaddaya

Listen to the short conversation. Which do you hear: *What do you*, *What are you*, **or** *What have you*? **Circle the correct words.**

1. MALE #1: What are you doing?
2. MALE #2: Nothing. What do you have in mind?
3. MALE #1: Well, what are you watching on TV?
4. MALE #2: It's almost 8:00 P.M. What do you think I'm watching?
5. MALE #1: I don't know. What have you decided to watch?

Test 9: *'ave/*'as/*'ad

Listen to the short conversation.

1. MALE #1: What have you done?
2. MALE #2: Nothing, I had just finished reading my book when I saw it. What has *she* done?
3. MALE #1: She's only three years old. What do you mean, "What has *she* done?" What have *you* done? You're supposed to be watching her.
4. MALE #2: What have *they* done? She had to draw on the wall. They didn't give her any paper.

Test 10: *shoulda/*shouldna
   *coulda/*couldna
   *woulda/*wouldna

Listen to the short conversation. Which do you hear: *should have*, *shouldn't have*; *could have*, *couldn't have*; *would have* **or** *wouldn't have*? **Circle the correct words.**

1. MALE: I should have just had coffee. I shouldn't have eaten those two pieces of pie and the rest of the cake.
2. FEMALE: You couldn't have eaten all of that!
3. MALE: Well, I did. I wouldn't have eaten the pie, but it was chocolate. I shouldn't have eaten the cake, too.
4. FEMALE: I couldn't have eaten all of that. I would have stopped after the pie.
5. MALE: I could have tried, but the cake was also chocolate.

Test Yourself Answer Key

Test 1: Do *ya/Are *ya

1. Do you
2. Are you
3. Do you
4. Do you
5. Are you

Test 2: *wanna/*gonna

1. want to
2. going to
3. going to
4. going to
5. want to
   want to

Test 3: *kin/can't

1. Can
2. can't
   can
3. can't
   can
4. Can
5. can't
   can

Test 4: *hafta/*hasta

1. have to
2. have to
   has to
3. has to
4. have to

Test 5: *'im/*'em

1. him
2. him
3. them
4. them
   them
5. him
   them

Test 6: *'n'/*er

1. and
2. or
3. And
   and
4. or
5. And
   or

Test 7: *er/*fer/*'er

1. her
   or
2. or
3. for
   or
4. her
   for
5. her

Test 8: *Whaddaya

1. What are you
2. What do you
3. What are you
4. What do you
5. What have you

Test 9: *'ave/*'as/*'ad

1. have
2. had
   has
3. has
   have
4. have
   had

Test 10: *shoulda/*shouldna *coulda/*couldna *woulda/*wouldna

1. should have
   shouldn't have
2. couldn't have
3. wouldn't have
   shouldn't have
4. couldn't have
   would have
5. could have

Chapter Answer Key (Part 2, Practice)

1. How's Your Family? (*yer)
Practice, Page 3

1. your	3. you're	5. your	7. your	9. your	11. You're
2. You're	4. You're	6. your	8. your	10. Your	12. You're

2. Yours Is a Great Job! (*yers)
Practice, Page 6

1. yours	3. You're	5. Your	7. yours	9. Yours	11. Yours
2. Your	4. yours	6. Yours	8. Your	10. you're	

3. I Have the Perfect Car for You (*fer)
Practice, Page 9

1. for	4. You're	7. for	10. for	12. You're	14. for
2. For	5. for	8. Your	11. for	13. for	15. your
3. For	6. for	9. For			

4. Where Are the Bags of Chips? (*a)
Practice, Page 12

1. You're	4. of	7. of	10. your	13. of	15. of
2. your	5. of	8. for	11. of	14. of	16. for
3. of	6. of	9. of	12. for		

5. Do You Like Artificial Intelligence (*ya)
Practice, Page 15

1. you	4. for	7. you're	10. you	13. you	16. you
2. you	5. you	8. You're	11. You're	14. of	
3. your	6. you	9. you	12. You're	15. you	

6. Let's Go Shopping (*in')
Practice, Page 18

1. you	6. for	10. of	14. For	18. taking	22. you
2. looking	7. your	11. your	15. going	19. of	23. You're
3. for	8. you	12. looking	16. going	20. wearing	24. standing
4. you	9. you	13. for	17. you	21. for	25. of
5. looking					

7. What Are You Doing This Weekend? (*Whaddaya)
Practice, Page 21

1. what	6. you	10. you	14. yours	18. jumping	22. what
2. do	7. having	11. drinking	15. you	19. What	23. are
3. you	8. what	12. of	16. What	20. do	24. you
4. What	9. are	13. of	17. do	21. you	25. writing
5. do					

8. I Want to Have a Hamburger (*wanna)
Practice, Page 24

1. What	7. to	13. want	19. to	24. you	29. for
2. do	8. want	14. to	20. you	25. want	30. of
3. you	9. to	15. want	21. want	26. to	31. you
4. want	10. What	16. to	22. to	27. for	32. you
5. to	11. do	17. of	23. of	28. your	33. you
6. want	12. you	18. want			

9. We're Going to See "The Monster That Ate Cleveland" (*gonna)
Practice, Page 28

1. what	7. to	13. going	19. you	25. you	31. to
2. are	8. You	14. you	20. going	26. going	32. want
3. you	9. you're	15. want	21. to	27. to	33. to
4. going	10. of	16. to	22. of	28. want	34. your
5. to	11. going	17. What	23. want	29. to	35. want
6. going	12. to	18. are	24. to	30. going	36. to

10. Can You See the Stage? (*kin, can't)
Practice, Page 31

1. Can	8. Can	14. What	20. Can	26. playing	32. can't
2. you	9. you	15. are	21. you	27. can't	33. Can
3. can't	10. going	16. you	22. you	28. you	34. you
4. of	11. to	17. saying	23. enjoying	29. can't	35. for
5. of	12. playing	18. can't	24. Can	30. want	36. can
6. Can	13. you	19. you	25. you	31. to	37. you
7. you					

11. What Can I Get You for Your Cold? (*git)
Practice, Page 34

1. you	7. going	13. you	19. get	24. can	29. get
2. doing	8. to	14. Can	20. for	25. get	30. you
3. get	9. You're	15. you	21. get	26. you	31. Can
4. Can	10. for	16. get	22. yours	27. for	32. you
5. get	11. what	17. can	23. for	28. can	33. get
6. you	12. do	18. you			

12. Take Bus 4 to Second Street (*ta)
Practice, Page 37

1. you	8. you	14. to	20. are	26. to	32. to
2. to	9. for	15. What	21. you	27. get	33. to
3. To	10. What	16. do	22. going	28. to	34. get
4. you	11. do	17. you	23. to	29. of	35. of
5. to	12. you	18. to	24. want	30. Your	36. to
6. get	13. want	19. What	25. to	31. to	37. to
7. Can						

13. I'm Going to Try to Find a Job (*da)
Practice, Page 40

1. to	7. of	13. want	19. to	25. to
2. to	8. to	14. to	20. of	26. you
3. want	9. your	15. to	21. you	27. want
4. to	10. to	16. to	22. want	28. to
5. go	11. for	17. Can	23. to	29. to
6. to	12. you	18. you	24. to	30. for

14. I've Got to Check Your Teeth (*gotta, *hafta, *hasta)
Practice, Page 43

1. got	8. you	15. has	21. can	27. to	33. got
2. to	9. You	16. to	22. have	28. have	34. to
3. has	10. have	17. you	23. to	29. to	35. has
4. to	11. to	18. has	24. to	30. to	36. to
5. going	12. You	19. to	25. to	31. got	37. got
6. to	13. going	20. to	26. have	32. to	38. to
7. to	14. to				

15. She Used to Ride a Harley (*useta, *supposta)
Practice, Page 46

1. You	10. to	19. you	27. changing	35. used	43. to
2. can't	11. You're	20. to	28. for	36. to	44. supposed
3. for	12. You're	21. used	29. to	37. for	45. to
4. You	13. supposed	22. to	30. you	38. for	46. for
5. can't	14. to	23. supposed	31. of	39. used	47. supposed
6. supposed	15. You	24. to	32. you	40. to	48. to
7. to	16. used	25. supposed	33. used	41. to	49. of
8. want	17. to	26. to	34. to	42. used	50. to
9. to	18. to				

16. What's the Fastest Way to Send His Packages? (*'e, *'is, *'im, *'er, *'em)
Practice, Page 50

1. want	11. have	21. her	30. them	39. your	48. them
2. to	12. to	22. have	31. her	40. he	49. his
3. to	13. get	23. to	32. her	41. get	50. he
4. you	14. them	24. get	33. you	42. them	51. can't
5. want	15. him	25. to	34. them	43. for	52. his
6. to	16. What	26. he	35. him	44. his	53. going
7. them	17. do	27. has	36. you	45. him	54. to
8. sending	18. you	28. to	37. them	46. he	55. to
9. them	19. to	29. get	38. to	47. get	56. You're
10. to	20. her				

17. We Arrive on Tuesday and Leave on Thursday (*'n')
Practice, Page 54

1. and	8. Can't	15. you	21. and	27. and	33. and
2. singing	9. you	16. And	22. yours	28. Can't	34. you
3. and	10. him	17. can	23. And	29. and	35. can
4. playing	11. to	18. for	24. Can	30. and	36. and
5. singing	12. to	19. and	25. and	31. of	37. can
6. and	13. him	20. for	26. can't	32. and	38. to
7. playing	14. can't				

18. Do You Want a Chocolate or Lemon Birthday Cake? (*er)

Practice, Page 58

1. you	10. What	19. to	28. you	37. and	46. supposed
2. want	11. do	20. can't	29. your	38. You	47. to
3. to	12. you	21. you	30. or	39. them	48. your
4. or	13. or	22. or	31. can	40. you	49. or
5. you	14. you	23. your	32. you	41. get	50. you
6. want	15. going	24. And	33. or	42. your	51. can
7. to	16. to	25. you	34. you	43. You	52. you
8. want	17. of	26. What	35. to	44. can	53. to
9. to	18. got	27. do	36. your	45. you're	

19. I Don't Know What Classes to Take (*donno)

Practice, Page 62

1. you	9. to	17. don't	24. thinking	31. your	38. to
2. doing	10. You're	18. know	25. don't	32. don't	39. you
3. don't	11. what	19. you	26. know	33. know	40. you
4. know	12. do	20. want	27. you	34. you're	41. can
5. can	13. you	21. to	28. can	35. thinking	42. you
6. you	14. want	22. used	29. you	36. you	43. don't
7. don't	15. to	23. to	30. to	37. have	44. know
8. know	16. you				

20. Can't You Find an Apartment? (*cha, *cher)

Practice, Page 65

1. you	9. you	17. you	25. want	32. to	39. want
2. to	10. you	18. to	26. to	33. want	40. to
3. you	11. what	19. for	27. at	34. to	41. what
4. to	12. you're	20. of	28. your	35. aren't	42. you're
5. you	13. looking	21. you	29. and	36. you	43. looking
6. you	14. got	22. What	30. You're	37. don't	44. for
7. want	15. to	23. you're	31. going	38. know	45. or
8. to	16. don't	24. saying			

21. Could You Check My Sink? (*ja, *jer)

Practice, Page 68

1. your	8. your	15. to	22. You	28. Did	34. going
2. you	9. you	16. and	23. have	29. you	35. to
3. your	10. your	17. you	24. to	30. your	36. for
4. going	11. them	18. your	25. Can't	31. you	37. and
5. to	12. or	19. Would	26. you	32. you	38. Could
6. have	13. Your	20. you	27. them	33. can	39. You
7. to	14. have	21. to			

22. Who Have You Asked to Fly the Plane? (*'ave, *'as, *'ad)

Practice, Page 72

1. What	10. you	19. going	28. to	37. had	46. have
2. are	11. doing	20. to	29. has	38. don't	47. you
3. you	12. jogging	21. You	30. he	39. know	48. to
4. doing	13. playing	22. used	31. to	40. you	49. has
5. have	14. and	23. to	32. he	41. he	50. taking
6. you	15. to	24. have	33. had	42. to	51. her
7. have	16. have	25. to	34. you	43. has	52. you
8. what	17. you	26. have	35. and	44. his	53. want
9. have	18. to	27. you	36. he	45. to	54. to

23. Could I Have an Appointment with Dr. Okamoto? (*'ave, *'as, *'ad *'aven't, *'asn't, *'adn't)

Practice, Page 76

1. you	11. to	20. you	29. you	38. He	47. hasn't
2. have	12. your	21. your	30. You're	39. had	48. for
3. had	13. to	22. for	31. saying	40. to	49. for
4. your	14. you	23. have	32. have	41. you	50. You're
5. want	15. to	24. can't	33. of	42. have	51. going
6. to	16. have	25. you	34. did	43. for	52. to
7. to	17. of	26. had	35. you	44. He	53. have
8. your	18. to	27. get	36. your	45. has	54. to
9. haven't	19. Can	28. have	37. Playing	46. He	55. for
10. listening					

24. I Shouldn't Have Had Three Pieces of Cake (*shoulda, *coulda, *woulda, *musta, *maya, *mighta, *shouldna, *couldna, *wouldna)

Practice, Page 80

1. you	6. have	11. stopping	16. using	21. you	26. You
2. smoking	7. burning	12. smoking	17. would	22. could	27. couldn't
3. You	8. You're	13. You	18. have	23. have	28. have
4. you	9. shouldn't	14. should	19. working	24. may	29. your
5. must	10. have	15. have	20. for	25. have	

25. What Are You Doing to My Hair? (*Whatcha)

Practice, Page 84

1. what	11. to	20. doing	29. You're	38. to	47. cutting
2. are	12. to	21. you	30. going	39. to	48. You
3. you	13. you're	22. or	31. to	40. got	49. to
4. doing	14. and	23. What	32. don't	41. to	50. what
5. doing	15. you	24. are	33. know	42. them	51. have
6. what	16. you	25. you	34. What	43. What	52. you
7. you	17. you	26. taking	35. are	44. are	53. to
8. to	18. what	27. or	36. you	45. you	54. to
9. cutting	19. you're	28. you	37. going	46. doing	55. of
10. your					

26. Give Me a Paintbrush (*lemme, *gimme)

Practice, Page 88

1. want
2. to
3. you
4. to
5. to
6. to
7. to
8. of
9. used
10. to
11. You
12. don't
13. know
14. Let
15. me
16. You
17. Give
18. me
19. Give
20. me
21. get
22. want
23. to
24. get
25. Let
26. me
27. you
28. Give
29. me
30. of
31. Give
32. me
33. get
34. give
35. me
36. Let
37. me
38. You're
39. Let
40. me
41. yours
42. You
43. you
44. What
45. have
46. you
47. your
48. of
49. Let
50. me
51. used
52. to

27. I Couldn't Take the Test Because I Was Sick (*'bout, *'cause, *c'mon)

Practice, Page 92

1. you
2. going
3. have
4. to
5. because
6. of
7. Come
8. on
9. have
10. to
11. you
12. About
13. you
14. have
15. to
16. get
17. because
18. want
19. to
20. get
21. want
22. to
23. to
24. have
25. have
26. to
27. because
28. You're
29. working
30. for
31. about
32. get
33. have
34. to
35. have
36. to
37. come
38. on
39. going
40. to
41. got
42. to
43. to
44. because
45. got
46. to
47. get
48. you
49. About
50. you
51. you

28. Been to the Circus Lately? (Deletions of Words in Questions)

Practice, Page 96

1. want
2. you
3. to
4. going
5. to
6. to
7. meet
8. you
9. and
10. Do
11. you
12. Want
13. to
14. You
15. Don't
16. you
17. don't
18. know
19. Would
20. you
21. Like
22. to
23. have
24. you
25. seen
26. to
27. Come
28. on
29. you
30. to
31. them
32. to
33. him
34. Do
35. you
36. Know
37. want
38. to
39. want
40. to
41. Are
42. You
43. going
44. to
45. Do
46. you
47. Want
48. to
49. you

29. Where Are Your Extra-Large Hats? (Unusual Contractions)

Practice, Page 100

1. For
2. To
3. to
4. you
5. Where
6. will
7. connect
8. you
9. to
10. Can
11. you
12. Where
13. are
14. your
15. going
16. to
17. have
18. to
19. you
20. to
21. Can
22. you
23. where
24. will
25. Let
26. me
27. you
28. to
29. you
30. Why
31. are
32. your
33. What
34. are
35. you
36. looking
37. Where
38. will
39. them
40. have
41. to
42. you
43. to
44. Why
45. will
46. have
47. to
48. to
49. to
50. them
51. talking
52. to
53. your
54. What
55. will
56. have
57. to
58. to
59. you
60. to
61. can
62. you
63. Your
64. to
65. can't

30. When Will Your TV Program Be Over? (Unusual Contractions)

Practice, Page 104

1. When
2. are
3. you
4. going
5. to
6. your
7. watching
8. When
9. will
10. want
11. to
12. What
13. do
14. you
15. want
16. to
17. going
18. to
19. of
20. talking
21. about
22. You
23. supposed
24. to
25. How
26. are
27. supposed
28. to
29. You
30. have
31. you
32. Who
33. are
34. you
35. kidding
36. have
37. to
38. How
39. will
40. got
41. to
42. Who
43. will
44. can't
45. got
46. to
47. Have
48. you
49. Seen
50. of

Alternate Levels of Reductions

The pronunciation levels will be shown as Levels 1, 2, 3, and 4.

Example:

Chapter	Level 1: *Slowest*	Level 2: *Slow*	Level 3: *Faster*	Level 4: *Fastest*
9	going to + verb	going *ta	*gonna	*'onna (only after "I'm")

In my research, which consisted of recordings of unscripted speech by highly educated native English speakers, Level 1 speech occurred 8 times, Level 2 reductions occurred 47 times, and Level 3 reductions occurred 258 times.

Therefore, when there is more than one level of reduction possible, *Whaddaya Say? Third Edition*, focuses on Level 3 reductions, which are the most common.

Chapter	Level 1	Level 2	Level 3	Level 4
7	What do you	*Whadda you	*Whaddaya	
	What do { we / they }	*Wha do { we / they }	*Whadda	
	What are you	*What're *ya	*Whaddaya	
8	want to	want *ta	*wanna	
9	going to + verb	going *ta	*gonna	*'onna (only after "I'm")
13	to after vowel sound	*ta	*da	
14	got to	got *ta	gotta	
	have to	have *ta / haf to	*hafta	*'afta
	has to	has *ta	*hasta	*'asta
15	used to	used *ta	*useta	
	supposed to	supposed *ta	*supposta	*s'posta
20	/t/ + you	*ya / *chou	*cha	
	/t/ + your, you're	*yer	*cher	
21	/d/ + you	*ya / *jou	*ja	
	/d/ + your	*yer	*jer	
22	What have you	What *'ave you	What *of you	*Whaddaya
	What have { we / they }	What *'ave	What *of	*Whadda
23	Subject + have	*'ave	*of	
24	modals + have + past participle	should *of / could *of (etc.)	*shoulda / *coulda (etc.)	
25	What are you	What *chou	*Whatcha	

Sentence Blending Rules

The reductions taught in this book generally focus on pronunciation changes at the word level. However, there are other types of pronunciation changes that occur at the phrase or sentence level. "Blending" is an example. There are many sentence blending rules, but these three are the most common and useful.

1. Linking with Vowels

When a word ends with a consonant sound and the next word begins with a vowel sound, we often link the sounds by moving the consonant sound to the vowel sound. Speakers typically link/blend sounds in this way when the speaker continues talking after the blended sounds. Say the following examples without pausing after each word.

Examples: Ca<u>n</u> <u>i</u>t work?
Doe<u>s</u> <u>i</u>t work?
I<u>s</u> <u>i</u>t ready?
Co<u>me</u> <u>on</u>. We're late.

2. Linking Identical Consonants

When the end of one word has the same sound as the beginning of the next word, English speakers only pronounce the identical sound once if the words are pronounced without pausing. Say the following examples without pausing after each word.

Examples: bee<u>n</u> <u>n</u>o

goo<u>d</u> <u>d</u>eal

fel<u>t</u> <u>t</u>ired

thi<u>s</u> <u>s</u>eat

3. The Flap Sound

When /t/ occurs between vowels (a vowel sandwich), it's pronounced as a flap. The sound is similar to a fast /d/ – the tongue touches the front gum ridge (the part of the roof of your mouth behind your top teeth) very quickly.

Examples: a l<u>ot</u> <u>of</u>

m<u>oto</u>r

Conversational Strategies

Conversational strategies are mostly informal words and phrases used in spoken English, but generally not in written English. Speakers use these informal expressions to maintain a conversation and show reactions and emotions.

Example:

Written English

Is the report ready? I need it right away.

Spoken English

Hey, is the…**uh**… report ready? I need it…**like**…right away.

Explanations are in parentheses below.

1. *Uh huh* (Yes)

2. *Unh unh* (No)

3. *Uh* (Gives the speaker time to think. Don't use this in your own speech too much. It weakens your speech if used too much.)

4. *Hmm* (I'm thinking.)

5. *Irregular pacing* (Spoken English isn't spoken at one uniform speed. When speakers speak faster, you can expect more reduced forms and sentence blending.)

6. *Uh oh* (Oh, no. There's trouble.)

7. *You know* (Gives the speaker time to think. Again, don't use this too much in your own speech.)

8. *Repetition of words* (Speech isn't written ahead of time, so sometimes people repeat words as they're thinking.)

9. *Hey* (An informal way to get attention. It can be rude.)

10. *Huh?* (An informal way to say "What?")

11. *In other words* (To restate what was already said)

12. *Sentence rephrasing* (Sometimes, speakers don't like what they started to say, so they abandon it and start a sentence they prefer. Example: I want to talk about . . . I'd like to say . . .)

13. *Ah* (I finally understand.)

14. *Oops, whoops* (I made a small mistake.)

15. *Let's see…* (Gives the speaker time to think)

16. *Like* (Using "like" when it has no meaning – i.e., using it as a "filler" word, not as a verb – lowers the sophistication of a sentence. If people are talking in more formal situations, such as in a job interview, they wouldn't want to use it. Example: "We went to… like… three places before we could like find what we needed." In this very informal example, "like" has no meaning.)

17. *Tsk tsk tsk* (Used to tease someone, to reprimand them for doing something they shouldn't do)

18. *Aha* (I've discovered something. "Aha! There are my keys. I thought I'd lost them.")